Mommy, Daddy are you Fine?

T*he Family Disputes Law 2023!*

(Foreword)

Welcome to this informative guide and support. In this book, you will be guided through the journey you may be experiencing. Through research, personal insight, and case studies you will discover what is out there to provide support throughout a most difficult time. Justin has been diligent in his research of the system, what to expect, and the many challenges you may face. The book prepares you for your journey and how to cope with everything that can and will occur. A very true and factual writing, with all the avenues of support and encouragement you need to help you on your path. Throughout it will prepare you for the court experience, and how it can affect you. But more importantly. Showing you are not alone.

THERE ARE ORGANISATIONS to help and assist and the whole process is explained in a heartfelt way, with empathy and compassion.

All the tools you need to deal with not only yourself but also the welfare of your loved ones. This book provides you with insights and all the many supportive organizations that are there to help.

A work filled with passion and reassurance for the reader that you are not alone!

(Preface)

We bring you through some of life's most important trials and tribulations, faced consequently within the injustice of things, that many parents and children struggle with today. To help you throughout this journey, I will set forth an appraisal of guided steps we can take to better the chances of the relationship between child and parent. You may feel that the system is very one-sided when it comes to giving who has access to your children, with Social Services, CaffCass & Child Maintenance Services. With all those odds they would've taken a review and taken into account that the children reside with the opposing parent, which has left you feeling with a lack of enthusiasm, lack of self-esteem, and a failure as a parent. I like you, haven't given up my observations against all odds that humanity is up against. But believe me, my compassionate heart is led to believe. That I can give you a better understanding of how to guide you through this situation. You may or may not even be this close to setting forth an application to the courts yet. I will provide you, with every single bit of information that you desire to start to set things straight, both as a parent and for your children's sake.

Introduction!

We introduce you to our guide review of what you can expect ahead of the journey to parent alienation and the psychological effects it has both on you and your offspring. This certainly is a discipline for the strong-minded and caring parent. Will set forth what to expect, with feelings, emotions, and the traumas you'll be up against. But through it all, you must be fully equipped with patience. This will explain every detail of how to apply to the courts, and what forms to fill out. You'll have to prioritize your life with an intellectual focus to proceed and make success on your own accord. Or you will be willing to have to pay for fortunate solicitor and court fees. I have several friends who had the same situation, business owners, who had to pay family judicial and solicitor fees of around £60,000 BS.

The Judicial Review won't necessarily be easy!

Through the injustice of things, we unfortunately need time and forbearance although it sounds unfair as the children are residing with the opposing parents. You are probably thinking in an ideological World, why isn't egalitarianism met to its standards yet? The psychological impairment has become a disparity for you and your children goes untold, careless, recklessly 9/10 cases become in the mother's favor. It is a traditional heritage over the archaic historical times, that Mothers have always been destined to be housewives and mothers to the children. Whilst a man/father is to carry out the man's duties, and hard labor, many have been soldiers or some form of a market society as that seems to become the norm. Like a macho thing for a man to approve himself to his wife/girlfriend, when we say a market society, it can also mean for example... Soldiers, footballers, rugby, boxing, and motorcycle racing. Where anything and everything is up for sale, putting your life at risk, like a monkey at a circus for others' entertainment. We are going to set forth a teleological precedent in how we can prioritize getting things into place, to give you a better opportunity. How to go about getting access to seeing your children once again!

(Chapter 1)

Building your Foundations!

Be prepared before you even contemplate applying to the courts, it's a long process, but ultimately a rewarding method as any child needs both parents. An offspring growing up wants and looks for answers, imagine being that child and one parent had to leave due to a relationship breakdown, birthdays, Christmas, and school holidays. Where you used to be there for them, guide them, and encourage them. When a child loses that, they lose direction and stability. Your absence is just as fundamentally damaging to them as it is to yourself. All those most cherishing responsibilities have been taken away from you and how you inspire them, they now don't have that legacy. It's morally not fair and unacceptable. As you lose your parental responsibility. You have more than likely felt a lack of self-esteem, suicidal thoughts, feelings of resentment, and a worthless, helpless parent. There is no worse label than being an alienated parent. What does it mean, incompetent, rejected by the system? Believe me, you're not on this journey alone. Absolute thousands within the United Kingdom are facing the same trials each day through the Family Courts, I have sat physically through many Court hearings where the father has lost his contact or trying to get joint contact and parental responsibilities. The objective is to grant you custody, you were given that responsibility by the mother when you both decided to have unprotected intercourse. So be more than encouraged, as I will make you flourish with hope and direction. Whilst you are thinking about the following steps to plan your journey, you have already taken the proper steps. But I am not going to sugarcoat it. I have seen many cases take anything from two years up to eight years, and you are also going to have to make some exquisite decisions, possibly sacrifices & adaptations. But hypothetically from a speaking point of view. As I don't personally know you and you don't know me. If it's changing how you live, or where you live. Changing your circles of friends for instance, then make those adaptations to better your circumstances. Which will then hold no ammunition for the opposing party to make things harder for yourself. Through social services, CaffCass and the Family Courts. Because believe me, each, and everything that you are dreading from the separation and stories from 1978, even if it was something as silly as throwing a penny sweet at your girlfriend or boyfriend's head, or you stayed at a friend's house. It will be exaggerated as much as possible to put a blockade in the way of your justice.

(Be prepared)

Start to get your life on track, simply because you don't want the perpetrator to make a statement, to try and deflect you as a responsible father/mother. In this World, you would've already discovered as each, and every person will become a judge at every point and direction you take in life, how you look, how you dress, your likes, dislikes, your work ethic, hobbies, interests. These judges will also take responsibility for how you've maintained yourself throughout life's trials and tribulations. And consider how you acted previously, in your hobbies, interests, and workplace, through those tasks you set out to do. Does this affect how you care, and love for your children as a father? Many people don't come to realize the compassion an alienated father or father, has for their child! But most of all what does prove that you have the will to keep applying pressure through the Court system until they can analyse it's not you failing as a father or mother. It's the Justice within the system and the lack of support to grant your honest validation as a parent back. In a breakdown of a family relationship, they usually consider 9/10 times it is the father's fault because men are frowned upon when owning up to physical abuse, and mental abuse, by their baby's mother. It also is a tradition that fathers go out to work to support themselves and the family because girlfriends or wives become household maids or housewives. The working parent, I mean today you see so many working-class mother's others also, such as my mother, sister, aunts, etc. We're growing up, but traditionally throughout historic times and some still today have many men within each household being the man of the house, most men are born to hard labor, in all weather conditions, rainstorms, and snowstorms. Working all the hours under the sun, alone has such a detrimental effect, on low self-esteem, and lack of self-worth, and makes you feel like you have zero duty as a boyfriend, husband, or father. These working environments become displeasing, so the working gang comes Friday after a horrendous working week and ends up during unsociable hours at their local working club, this is displeasing to his girlfriend/wife and children. But many men face the trial of going home to their wife or girlfriend to be moaned at, going out shopping after a long day's graft at work, and yes plenty of nagging. When all they want is for someone to understand the treacherous conditions, they put themselves through, and to contribute towards his family also. I have no idea who you are, the reader, or the person you were or want to become. But you were a father, and still are. But you will have to put yourself straight, make a change, and be very prepared for, what is to come. Don't become antagonized by what is said on behalf of your ex-partner, mother, or father to your child. You'll find Social Services will always take sides of where the kids are residing at the current. Both Social Services and CaffCass will do a background check. Don't panic because you can prove to be better than your past, as no breakup in a relationship is nice. Both me, you, and them all know having a family taken away from you is almost like a death sentence. This is why I say it takes time and forbearance, preparation, to prove yourself. Are you happy with what you got now? Could you change as a better person, have a better vision, and set a better example? You need to think, are you cut out for all this? simply because thousands of broken families are in the same position as you! They will take the mother's position in all this, as the children are with her and her new partner. The mother won't like you moving on and letting her and your children meet your new lady. You want to cry for egalitarianism, a fair-trade system, you both move on, both parents understand and bring the children up like normal broken-down families?

(Unfortunately, the Law is not Scientifically prepared for realism or what we call a fair-trade system of sexes) So like I say be very prepared that the system of things is not just, it cannot always be fair, but be very prepared to, put up a fight. It's easy for the courts if you go and hang yourself, or drink yourself to death down the pub. The fight you're only putting up with is endurance, integrity, and wisdom to prove that you are better than that. With hope one day your kids will grow up, they will like you someday go through all the emotions you have, with relationships, and have children of their own. You are your children's legacy, should you go and get married again, have more children, go down the pub get wasted with friends, take narcotics? Don't get me wrong there is a whole wide world out there to enjoy, maybe you can get married again someday and enjoy sharing love with another again, but right now your kids should be your priority. We are made to love the opposite sex, of course, let's just say in some cases. We ought to have those thoughts, but initially, our focus is always on our children. We know this because our consciousness tells us, these things. That's a guilty feeling, that you're letting not just yourself down again, but also your children. But right now, we are going to make a plan to get access through the Family Court, by implying to the examples that Social Services and CaffCass a good well-being, vitality, and Mental health, in a good standing order. Don't be too overwhelmed if you have had a mental breakdown in the past due to a relationship break up, it's very common. Even more a woman is likely to leave her boyfriend or husband, if he is no longer able to provide for his family due to health reasons, deterioration through age-related manual labor, blood conditions, diseases, muscular damage, or other health problems. This is when you need to set a vision for your future, make changes to become a better example, and show that you have a legacy for your children to become inspired, by you as a parent! Children imitate what is put in front of them, so make sure it's a positive change, so Social Services, CaffCass & the Family Courts can only approve you as a responsible caring adult.

Starting to visualize. What would help you keep focused? And make your children become inspired by the changes you can make that they can only benefit from. Set an appraisal of what could be, rather than what should be. We need to emasculate ideas, 1) set insight business realistic business goals, and relationships around your children 2) self-assessment, where are you at now? What could be done to improve the situation? 3) Analysing the situation, what needs to be changed? What's the focus? How can I go about doing it better? 4) Imitate? Who do you want to imitate? 5) Make an exquisite decision, finding a business goal perhaps that works around you, your family, your relationship, or marriage, finding the right marriage or relationship that works for the best of you, them, and your family.

In a correlation of all the distress, between yourself, the child/children. Although you feel that it is all the mother's/Father's fault for antagonizing the situation by keeping the children away from you to hurt/torment you as a father/mother depending on who the alienated parent is. This is likely the case and the fear of your bringing your child up around another partner perhaps or quite frankly through control or even out of spite. We are also on the understanding that a toxic relationship can cause a partner to leave as adequately, you would not only want happiness for your children/child but ultimately your health and safety are paramount. There is no reason to suggest this through the family judiciary or anything tactical, what best pleases the judge, is the parent who shows up, in a calm respectful, and timely manner. Write your statement, and prepare it well in advance, just regarding what you would like within the outcome between you and your child, children's future. The chances of you getting legal aid through solicitors are very unlikely even more so if she has got a non-molestation order against you, as this will go against you trying to apply for legal aid. Questions you will be asked! Whether that be CaffCass, Social Services, or the judge, possibly all three, will ask you what sort of relationship, you as a parent have with your children. The opposing parent may or may not have already been asked these questions, how were you around the children as a parent, were you caring, loving, providing, taking them to and from school, preparing meals for your child/ children? Don't let the thought of this already being brought before your attention to the parent residing with your child/ children. This can have a counterbalance to your psychological disorder and deteriorate things for you, trying to set your story straight. You need a clear consciousness, a clear mind to not let all these things disturb you, as they do this purposely to indirect your path. If you were to do your etiquette research from the year 2022, there were 2968 single parents (Clarke, 2023) D Clarke has done some social scientist analysis which gives us data on those who are single-parent family homes. From 1996 to 2022 years, with 2012 statistics being the year highest 3,039 single-family homes in the United Kingdom.

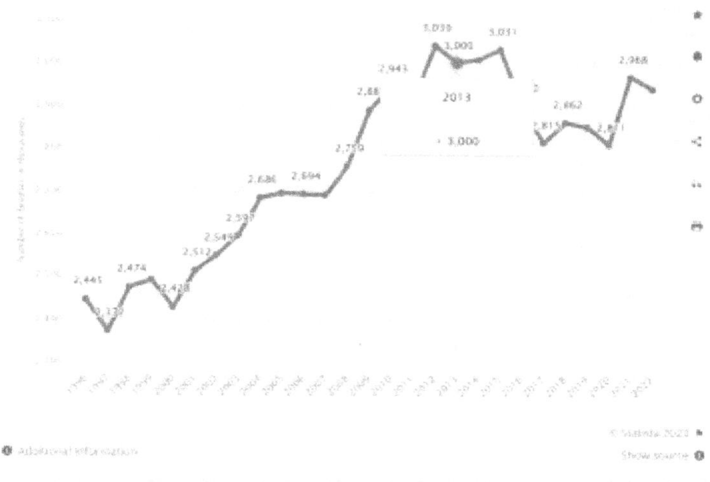

Number of single parent families in the UK 1996-2022

So, with this data analysis, across the whole spectrum of the United Kingdom, you need to start to visualize that you are not the only one facing the injustice of parenting. Take on your understanding, that these things need perseverance, patience and more importantly having the will to become an intellectual correspondent, rather than trying a more erratic tactical approach, through physical or verbal to make yourself known as true towards the perpetrator's perception of you, as a bad parent as that then becomes apparent as factual within its evidence! Sometimes we have to dig deeper into quantitative data research as we cannot always trust the publication for factual evidence, so here we can compare and contrast data analysis which will more than likely vary with collective data.

(Gingerbread, 2023)

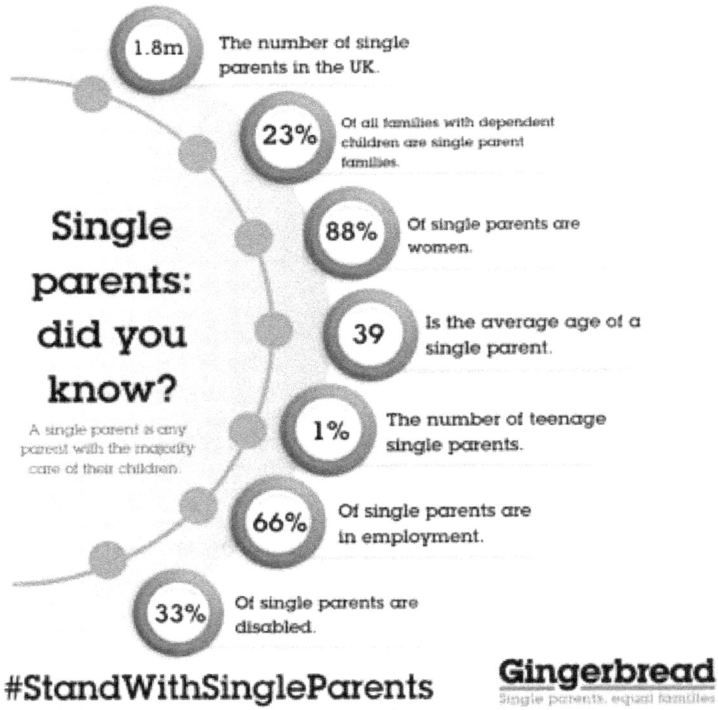

This collective data analysis was drawn to our attention by Lewisham's Gingerbread Single Parents Group, which is significantly a tallied total much larger than previous research of a total of 1.8 million single parents in 2013. Sparingly the most precious gift any mother and father can have is their offspring. You can work your whole working life trying to support your children, the negative defects of your breakdown in a relationship not only affect you as a parent but also your child. So, it's certainly best to make very positive steps and sacrifices, no matter how long it takes whether it's a couple of years or fifty years, so you need to be physically, and mentally prepared to set these foundations that will benefit your happiness, it doesn't necessarily mean financially prepared, preparing your welfare, wellbeing, and mentality. Being a lover of money can cause several altercations, such as overeating, alcoholism, or narcotics abuse. You need to find your niche, hobbies, and interests that will help you improvise to a positive change, bare in mind some hobbies, workplaces, and interests bring bad custom, so with that appraisal set before a positive but focused changed, only you can justify what works best for your mental health and vitality because overall this is what will be looked into moving forward. The family law system is unjust, or justice usually fits moulded around injustice, the religious bible already foretold that Satan would take the lead to the many of the World. But your story is to set things straight with complete purity and to give your child a caring, encouraging positive father, or mother.

Within the heights of a Judiciary and its legislation, they withheld a textbook strategy also known as the triangle.

The Victim/Alienated parent & Child

The Rescuer/Legislator

The Perpetrator/ The Parent with child.

It does have tactical ability, as the legislator is supported by reports from CaffCass and Social Services reports, they will try to delve into your past/History, of any medical, medication, or any treatments you have had previously. But don't panic as everyone faces different trials and tribulations throughout life's struggles. What you need to focus on right now is a positive structure that supports your wellbeing, mentality, and vitality. There is nothing more encouraging than a positive focused parent, rather than a rich parent, because the richest man in the world doesn't necessarily mean he is the wealthiest/healthiest man in the world, simply because the richest man in the world, has the wealthiest and healthiest heart and that doesn't cost a thing, that's just wisdom and knowledge, from Mental health, well-being & vitality.

When you are in your solace place, it will become time to reminisce about all those grandeur moments that you had spent with your child, it will be worthwhile taking note of those memories! Through fault or no fault of your own as you were vacant through the injustice of things and all the drastic calculations that have so far not been in your favour. It'll be worthwhile either speaking to Social Services or Caff Cass, of writing to your child/children or they may quite possibly have a contact arrangement, but doubtable, they may also not agree to either, so having said that you may Have to make an agreement by the Family Court Judge about contact, on the approach of contact it will pay dividends to have a focus on your child's/children hobbies/interests and all the things they like, ask them their favourite TV Programme, sports they enjoy, favourite place of interest, favourite landmark, best movie to watch, favourite colour. This will not only build on your relationship, but also show that you're focusing on all the things they like, which approved nurturing, caring father/ mothers response, as they may only remember the break up throughout the relationship with parent taking you responsibility, either for their lack of interest, which may have led to a disposable argument. It may well pay you to mention to the judge in question, what insight your children have into special memories and moments that they had spent with you, you want these questions to be brought to your children, on neutral terms, away from any bad influences, the opposing parentings family. You will find a different outcome, a positive outcome in a neutral environment, and a much more diverted outcome if the same question is asked about the child influencers, which is led by the perpetrator. You with have a negative outcome which shows only moral support to the adulting around those children at the time of responses.

Reasonable Facts

"Knowing your rights" as a parent. You and your ex-wife/gf/Husband/bf had consented sexual endeavours which gave you the most valuable cherishing gift, a man and woman could only wish for, regardless of your breakdown, the breakup of the relationship, marriage or even one-night stand in some cases, but let's say you became a responsible parent the moment you signed the birth documents, this doesn't necessarily mean you are the biological parent, although you want to agree to a lawful girlfriend or wife, let us take a

focus on writer "Mary

Wollstonecraft"(Wollstonecraft, 1993) (She was a

Feminist Philosopher and writer) with her Social Scientist perspective on male and female brain functioning, with the same traits, characteristics, and actions, In many of her writings although supporting women on a majority of occasions she shows her nobility and strength to encourage women equal to men, that is when you start to question the egalitarianism within the injustice of things as an alienated parent, how can we counterbalance and improve with evince with gender equalities? Making a start with improving Justice within parental responsibilities, the statistics encourage a child/ children growing up without their father's encouragement or lack of guidance, it proves today at a very large scale, a troublesome child, will move within a demographical society of sinful, lawless acts, such as high crime, thieving, narcotics, robbery, all these detestable things. All those responsible organisations (Social Services-CaffCass) so far have supported this divergence set for the perpetrator against the victim/ Alienated-Parent. Then the psychological impact it gives you as an alienated parent, makes you wonder! Are you facing being bribed, have they taken any constellation that the best interest of the children is to have support and encouragement from both parents? What is contemporary is the factual stimulation that is written in black and white Children Act 1989, however, are those fit for purpose stimulating its succession to approve an apostate, the judicial decision is never subsequently in favour of the alienated parent, rather they seem to analyse the response reports received by CaffCass and Social Services. But do not panic as with perseverance and understanding I will do my upmost best to set your journey straight with my guidance, support giving you supportive organisations that can not only give you moral support but the right guidance when facing Family trails.

JUST REMEMBER ITS OKAY not to be okay!

More importantly throughout this journey, in times of selfish hopelessness, lack of enthusiasm, and self-esteem. You will have moments of feeling incompetence, and distress, as an alienated parent is a label, which leaves you feeling emotionally distraught and a failure at times. But we have to look on the bright side, you now away from an unsatisfied relationship with your ex-spouse or partner. It's time to correct imperfections with a zeal of enthusiasm because already you're on the path to consolidating the fact that you are the apparent, caring parent to your offspring. It is a great idea to visualize an encompassing, encouraging, and compromising future for your legacy so that your children can be inspired and understanding, no matter what the outcome, you have left behind proven facts that your steady path wasn't the precedent of what the informer was tarnishing you out to be. You need to not let your opposing parent to your children, live in your head rent-free, otherwise your disposition will start to encompass negativity.

> Self-growth and Hatred feelings coming from resentment can likewise turn into a reason for not assuming command over our own lives and we can utilize our feelings of disdain to point the finger of fault at others for why we are not carrying on with the daily routine we need to experience. Resentment is most difficult when it is felt toward an individual, you are near, like a parent, old friend, or life partner.

If you do not beat sensations of feebleness, you could foster a negative, threatening disposition.

Hatred is extreme, particularly when you've been wounded by somebody profoundly.

We as a whole battle with disdain eventually in our lives. However, when we clutch outrage and disdain, it just goals us to experience more. What you may not understand is that disdain can significantly affect your physical and psychological wellness. Holding hard feelings makes us convey pessimistic, tense energy in our science.

"At the point when we clutch hard feelings and hatred, it resembles drinking poison and anticipating that the other individual should become ill. "You should focus on your degrees of hatred. Resulting in it being unrestrained and can harm you in additional ways than you know. The following are four diverse ways disdain influences your wellbeing. You need to make a stead-fast focus on positivity, the empowerment of men is genuinely a die-fast compromising situation, throughout traditional norms, when we exercise femininity through the judicial outcomes, the statistics and growth and problems caused are encompassing through supportive organisations, such as 'Social Services' and 'CaffCass', they do not take any consideration, of the children's, well-being, mental health, physical journey, all they desire is the parenting apparent to the children at the time of Court appearance with already favouritism and one-sided agreement. What any child or adult wants to hear from their parent is how much their alienated parent, really does actually 'love' and care for their spouse. And their parent is trying their upmost best to find amenable, but comprehensive foundations to build something constructive, regardless of money it is what matters most, the heart and compassion that any alienated parent has and shows, many who, take their pain into unsocialised alcoholism, narcotics, turning into crimes and gang-related crimes. Is that generally what they ought to come from their alienated parent, or letting the residing parent with the children, try to tarnish the other as an unsolicited, incompetent parent? I mean when will all the egotistical, bribing, tactical, and backbiting stop, and correspond with egalitarianism?

Please bare, in mind that being able to manage any Court scenario is highly frustrating, the build-up of feelings of anxiousness. Days and months before you've prepared and visualised everything that is, literate that you would want to bring before the judge and your ex-partner and how you would like to spend time with your offspring. By rights and by a family Judiciary you would think by now, that the battle with lawlessness would prioritize bringing families back together. However, in most cases, this is still irrelevant even so in today's modern society, the suicide rate has in time risen to the highest in decades. Like I said before 9/10 they? The /judge/ social-services/CaffCass will always consider the well-being of the mother and offspring before they even give you a thought. Just know that you will have to make yourself apparent, not by being verbally, abusive, outspoken, or by telling all you have achieved out of life. But by turning up to every single Court hearing. This will not only prove that you are very dedicated, but that you are adamant that you want to father your children. This will also provoke the opposing parent, let's just say the mother for this instance/mother as she is residing with the children, your offspring's. She will become aggravated, this will indicate your children, your children will be asking the mother questions. when she is upset. she will speak. Your children will soon find out how much you care and the love you have for them. You don't give up until justice has answered all your prayers. No matter what false allegations, in some sense, maybe true allegations. There is always two sides to every story, and the opposing parent will use every single ammunition, true or false to try and stop you in your path. You may find that they have family members acting as advocates to support their story, to try and force you into denial. The only witness you need is your consciousness, your heritage, and your DNA. You have oxygenated blood that pumps around your body from your heart/aorta, now listen up you keep fighting the good fight through the courts until your heart gives up. Again, not physically, or verbally abusive, but with an antagonizing righteousness. 'What's right is right, and justice will be done'. Always remember the bright side of life, they were happy when you always showed up, and they cannot take that away from you. Now that you're not there and you want what's equally right sharing parental responsibility, they don't want to show up, but Child Maintenance Services show up in your bank statement, 'A fair trade system' should be, you give a little you take a little! You pay (CMS) You see your children every other weekend, ultimate birthdays, Christmas' end of story.

THE TELEOLOGICAL THOUGHTFUL purpose of an alienated parent!

TROUBLESOME FACING (Child maintenance services!

Many alienated parents will argue the case, how can they pay for a child they are not willing to help fight through the courts to see their children, whilst having to pay (CMS) it may well be worthwhile to ask for DNA, as whilst yourself and your child/children are feeling some sort of interconnectedness, it wouldn't be the wrong thing to do, not to label the opposing parent. But also to give you answers to why you have been out of contact with your children. I have seen and witnessed a few cases where a gentleman was down for five years imprisonment for not paying Child Maintenance Services funds, for his alleged son by secret affair away from his wife with another lady, five years prior to his release he was trialed in another judicial hearing. He had asked on these occasions for approval of a legitimate DNA example to be taken, not to probe against his alleged son or secret affair, but to make an inquiry about his five years imprisonment. The Court trail continues, the mother to his son is adamant he is the father during the Court appearance, stating how such a horrific father figure he has been and how selfish and worthless he was to not be owning up to his responsibilities. Admittedly it's not nice for any teenage child to witness these sorts of scenarios that have happened in any court situation, but I like the rest of any alienated parenting situation. Would feel the necessary to reason why you had that bond taken away from yourself. Many people are at the arrival of this court appearance which was taking place in a U.S. Court, this man had been found guilty of not paying (Child Maintenance Services) payments, done his five years in prison, these people hearing the court hearing in the attendee seated area wasn't about to support this father of making a right decision about asking for DNA, they all had jumped to the conclusions, that he was a selfish, worthless parent. I mean these sorts of situations can happen to the best of us if we don't get honest answers. In today's modern society, you cannot trust anyone. So in that case, the father made the right choice to ask for DNA test to be done by High Court officials, The judge calls out the DNA examples, Mr_ _ _ _ _ _, you are on the birth certificate named as the responsible father to your son.

Prior to your imprisonment you were a father for eight years on and off and spent the last five years in prison, now you have spent your time on release you're asking for DNA Results.

(The Judge) Kkkk, I need to take a moment, I just need to clarify something with the mother before I reveal the answer, excuse me mam, do you honestly claim that MR_ _ _ _ _, is the father to your son? Absolutely she says to the judge, a lousy, sleazy father, never raised a hand in his pocket, he has never been there to support his son, through birth, the upbringing through until his teenage years, he was just non-existent a worthless man. Let's bare in mind as a tradition many men, not all, are made to be the breadwinners for their family. Well not quite the situation with this case anyhow, it was a secret affair, which led this mother to give this man a responsibility to father their alleged son,

(The Judge) is ready to reveal the answer... About those DNA Results, you made a statement that MR_ _ _ _, is the father to your teenage son, he's just lost five years of freedom due to imprisonment, do you realise the importance of getting this right to who is the father to your son, And by a way of right's we are about to tell you, that MR_ _ _ _, is not the father to your son..

This story is based on a real-life scenario, court hearing which can be found on (YouTube), I watched it several months ago, I also talk and observe many other alienated father and mothers across the World which face very similar situations. Of paying large amounts of sums of monies into (Child Maintenance Services) and still not being able to see their children.

Here is an example, that I paraphrased and observed through a social media application, such as Facebook, Child maintenance services for alienated parents.

'A chap was talking about his ex-partner' After tricking me into getting a visa, she ran away and asked me to pay 600 pounds a month to support the children and called her a prankster.

Before that, she was always violent, even

threatening to stab me once. When I refused to pay £600, she sent abusive messages which made me ignore her. I didn't bother looking for her or finding out where they were going because I just wanted my peace, my sanity, and my sanity intact. When she moved out, I asked the mover where he would help them move, But he said she told them not to tell me so he couldn't.

Covid happened and I sent her £50 on two separate occasions because that was how much I could afford as a full-time student, but she sent it back to me with insults. After that, I never bothered again until CM joined in September. I want my son, but the stress I have seen people go through just to see their child, CM, and their ex manipulate them and make many false allegations against NRP has made me scared to go down that path. My job, in particular, requires me to be clean and of good character, as any unwarranted issues or accusations could cost me my career. What I know my ex is capable of

For example, when I disputed CM's advance payment due to a child living abroad that I raised, the matter went to court and I submitted a statement from my child's mother living abroad, she replied that it was a fake document and so was she. . lied that she tried many times to get me into my son's life, which was also a lie because I never received an email, call or text from her for 3-4 years remaining.

The only message I received from her was a letter about 1 year ago or February this year asking me to confirm that she had sole custody, but I ignored it because I knew that my UK visa She needs an extension and she wanted to use that!

You are not the only one in this situation, So I have utilized some useful information so you can compare and contrast evidence. Yes, he is a caring father he's paying (CMS), but he is stuck between a rock and a hard place here. Ideally, the father would want to go searching for his son in another country, as suggested he would sacrifice his job position and more than likely come back to his home Country lose his job, lose his house, and apartment, and more than likely be a civil dispute in a foreign country, which could lead you going to prison depending on their laws. The mother more than likely has a great support network within that country already, hence her tactical manoeuvre. So, for many unreasonable, reasons you would be fighting a losing battle.

Do you think the Injustice of things is morally wrong? I mean would you pay for shopping that you couldn't possibly eat? No matter what the circumstances you would always love your children and support them financially, but they should also prioritize and support you to see your children also. Is it unjust, and the majority left with an emotional feeling of uncertainty with such proposed laws? They certainly need to navigate through the system of things and support alienated parents and children as any child growing up without either parent, can turn to gang-related crimes, narcotics abuse, or alcoholism, without encouragement from both biological parenting, also stated in social workers education package before graduating with a degree in their field of knowledge. The transparency of the family law is leaving such a delinquent unregulated organisation, which frustratingly would much rather follow traditional blueprints, such as paternalistic families. Where housewives are left to support the children, and men are made, forced into slave labour, or turn themselves into war merchants.

In some sense, it would be morally wrong for us to send the mother to your children out to war, or slave labour within a construction site. So, to coincide with what's been opposed to an egalitarianism let's prioritize a 'fair trade' system with equal parental responsibilities for both mother and the father, as any individual family would want what is best for their offspring.

Let's take the characteristics of mother and father. The biological parents.

Taking into consideration mothers' responsibility, she has her, caring side, loving side. Let's just say, some mothers not all, as each individual differ. A mother is very passionate about how their child feels, with their problems and emotions. But she will try to consider how their child feels and support their children to follow their hearts.

This is systematically why God created man and woman, to come as one, and have children together, because ultimately, they both share some very caring responsibilities, as you can see they cannot chemically balance without the other parent's guidance and care biologically.

Now take into consideration a father's responsibility and character, he influences and encourages his children. You can go to your father with problems, he will either influence you to do better or encourage you to become stronger. Many fathers will mostly support their children in sports activities, and help them grow to become wise and strong. Most fathers will also tell their children not to rush into relationships or marriage as they have uncertainty about their child's future, a mother would more than likely influence it all the more.

A Family Dispute!

Having a civil dispute, or disagreement with your ex-spouse. It is such a very genuine but also unjust situation to get yourself into, even more so being a male. As we are masculine, not necessarily stronger, or physically built the larger frame than a woman. Our deeper voice in an argument is rather alarming to people passing by or next-door neighbours. This would then aggravate the social norm within society, which to their morale standards, is quite possibly a chemical imbalance. So, in the interest of raising their concerns for your family's safety (children and this instance in consideration of right or wrong, your spouse), they would Call 999 to the scene of the disturbance. "Metropolitan Police" please, at number 9 North Finchsted Road, we can hear what seems to be an aggressive male shouting at his wife, with two young children screaming in the background, can you come to the assistance?

The Police have now been notified to the scene, and all they are aware of, is an aggressive male, this male for this instance, was shouting at his ex-partner in pain, as his ex-partner repeatedly kept punching him in the face. Well to the two police officers' notice, they have only witnessed the male shouting at the scene, they end up bursting through the front door, as they hear two children screaming. They end up striking the male to the floor with necessary force, without any understanding the innocent male has now allegedly been assaulted twice.

This innocent male, has now been tried in Court for domestic abuse, question, what for exactly? The fact that he got punched by his ex-partner, or the fact that police were also trying to hide the evidence of assaulting an innocent man.

"Sometimes it's best to walk away rather than get drawn into a fight as that will only be used against you and make things worse, don't let them have the power to trigger you anymore. Although you may see them try, just know what they're trying to achieve, others may not see it but don't stoop to that level. Enjoy the time you have the best you can. Don't take what they say personally, your ex-spouse, legal authority, just remember your consciousness' is more powerful than any authority, siding with favouritism, taking bribery, or supporting feminism, and that says a lot more about them than the character you are, as your resilience will always shine through and someday your children will see that for themselves"!

Many problems facing Parent Alienation!

Parental alienation is counterintuitive, and most of us have never learned what to do and what not to do to help our children. As a result, you don't know whether your actions to help your child will be effective or will make the situation worse.

Your child has been placed in a high-conflict situation in which your ex will punish them if they don't do what is asked, which is to belittle you and stop contacting YOU. Your child does not want to be in this situation, and it is very stressful for them. The behaviours they exhibit are calling for help and asking you to help them as much as possible so they can get through this. You are only human, and this experience is deeply painful for you as a parent. You are hurt, and you feel unfair and angry. You have your own need for love and a close connection with your child. You will be constrained in your ability to connect through many social norms in society, you will not be able to interact with friends in meetings, maybe through work-related activities, even more so during festive and holiday periods. You will find your work colleagues. traveling abroad with your family with your children, it will make you feel longing for the memories of you and your children, make you question the injustice that makes you feel so indignant that you will Start comparing and contrasting how you maintain. for example, your lifestyle is different from theirs. But when you get agitated, you start focusing on your own needs rather than what your child wants from you. This often results in your child being pushed away because you don't handle the situation as well as possible. This simply falls into the hands of strangers.

I know how difficult this is for you because I am one of them myself and I must try to reestablish a relationship with my children. The key to overcoming this challenge is to learn how you can best help your child and restore your own mental and emotional health. So, with my guidance, I can help you and your children overcome parental alienation. This will help you change your thinking and approach to alienation, which will change your personal experience and help you best help your child, it's a very traumatic situation for both you are your child/children, with many different formative ways to be able to approach this alienation.

Therefore, the alienating parent often isolates his/her child/children and makes them dependent and affiliated, so that the child/children feel hatred, and resentment towards the other, healthy parent. more mentally. activity, stemming from a narcissistic and manipulative parent. Your child may experience feelings of grief and guilt over having to reject the other parent. That means divorces involving parental alienation never come easy. Many mental health professionals say, even when parental alienation is detected, how traumatic it is to separate a child from an alienating/inappropriate parent. The child's therapist may or may not report this to the court. This must then be correlated with the therapist and the court, allies of pathological insanity. They can diagnose alienation but don't know how to solve it. As for reunification therapy (there is no standard procedure), it depends on the cooperation of the alienated parent, which is unlikely. Any involvement with the alienating parent can even make things worse as they escalate their hatred, alienating behaviour, lies, and manipulation.

Ideally, therapy sessions will include the alienated child and the target parent. But if the child studies alone, they may become more irritable and the situation may escalate, the alienated child imitates the alienated parent and confirms false accusations often saying "Keep the 'status quo' ' in the best interests of the child. . But no assessment will be effective if courts and mental health therapists cannot act, and we

need people who understand parental alienation, or it will be in vain. Since it is difficult for the alienated child to admit what is happening to them, given their psychological control source, they need space and distance. This would require a court order to protect the separation, but it is expensive and time-consuming, and parental alienation is difficult to prove. Either way, it's a child protection issue, not child custody, it's a mental health issue. (Carl Jung), the famous psychiatrist believed that we begin life as a blank canvas and our experiences gradually add colour to it. He introduced the concept that our mind is made up of two archetypes:

character and his own shadow. Persona, derived from the Latin word meaning "mask," represents the image we present to the world and how we want to be perceived. Our shadow aspects are the parts of ourselves that we learn to hide as we grow up, experience life, and learn the "rules" of right and wrong, and what actions to take. that we think we should hide in the dark. These hidden emotions can turn into "dark" emotions, which manifest as health problems, mood swings, fears, and mental health problems. It seems easier to ignore the shadows, but they continue to appear and grow until we face them. As Carl Jung said so well, "What we do not perceive will appear in the destiny of our lives." We all have dark and light sides. If we learn to accept our shadows and their origins, they will no longer frighten or overshadow our lives. We can embrace them/our wholeness. (Jung, 2023) Alienated parents and those who consider themselves stronger, more righteous, and better – including our leaders and governments – have erected a front to hide deep wounds' identity, trauma, victimhood and darkness. Until they heal, they cannot help others as they would like to believe. They often have hidden agendas and are looking for a saviour or support system. When we no longer fulfill their agenda, they move from victim status to abuser status and make us their target. The deeper the wound, the more ferocious the attack. Essentially, they fight against their own projections, against their shadows. We can try to practice loving abandon when we find ourselves in this violent situation, especially towards alienated children. Sending our love. Be loving. Try to be happy. We must not let the judgments and opinions of others define our identity; they just define themselves. Many people are unable to see beyond their hurt and suffering and operate from this dark place. We can heal our shadow aspects and love ourselves to love others better.

Before we pass on to the next chapter, let us reflect on what we have covered and why I have

covered the contents, well firstly mainly to give you a discipline so you will be on the understanding of what you will not only be facing, but to give you a focus, a compassion to know that you are not the only one who are facing these such trials, some rather peculiar than others, what is supposed to be fair and what is fair, doesn't always seem to calculate to what we deem as right, or quite frankly what a family judiciary psychiatrist would seem fair on the perspective on the moral principles of both alienating parenting and children. There don't seem to be any virtuous examples of what could be a good parenting responsibility when they deem one parent away from their offspring, as suggested above both mother and father play a very responsible important role in their child's upbringing, just because x, y, or z didn't work out between both parents within the relationship, shouldn't then compel the other parent to separate their offspring from the other. Additionally, the focus of 'social services, CaffCas' primarily should respond to the matter of the importance to all parties' psychiatrists, well-being, in-aid both parenting responsibilities and more of bridging the gap separately to both parents, having played their part at different times at being a parent to their child/children, more on talking about the benefits of both their parenting skills. Encouragement, wisdom, integrity, and all the rights, wrongs, relationships, and life general walks throughs, to give the children the best influence from both worlds. I cannot encompass more of an ideological sense of the parent alienation system if I tried. However, bribery, backbiting, backstabbing, and many more controversial evince happen within these situations on a day-to-day basis. By God's grace I hope that the kingdom of lawlessness isn't apparent forever, by all means, the day of judgment will become, and those who pose against your existence shall be condemned along with the wicked.

On the thought of transparency between the judiciary, social services, and CaffCass terminology, is when you start to sit and beg to differ if they are partial between a correlation between not setting straight this battle of lawlessness your facing, I mean as I have shown above in previous diagrams/chart, the number of single parents, alienated parents and children amongst the United Kingdom is rather astonishing, abysmal behaviour when you come to think of the legal authorities assistance amongst things. Legal Solicitors are not making things any easier as they charge something in the region of £250 an hour, and that's just to read through the Court papers, family proceedings can take as we have witnessed from anything up to two years to ten years, I quoted myself a solicitor which I am facing the same trials as yourself, six years of court papers, four hours readings that are a sum of £1000, that's without her response to the courts, that's without her time spent with you through the trials.

Listen and I mean take note; predominantly you seriously need to be equipped, physically, mentally, and emotionally prepared. This could be possibly the hardest and longest storm you can ride. But most of all every time you're writing to the courts, turning up to court hearings, this is not only draining for you but also for the mother, this will signal the children. Don't give up until your heart gives out, unfortunately, if her heart gives out before yours, that's not

your fault she was trying to shield those children from the person she had chosen to have her offspring with. Your mind is driven to overtime.

'thinking' what has she been hiding, she's moved on with a new partner, most relationships as we know have insecurities, trials, and tribulations from both sides of the family, every opposing mother in law, or father in law, becomes the circuit overseer from a biased perspective from the relationship side of things, this will cause animosity, a disturbance between your ex-partner and new relationship,

which entails your children, allegedly affecting their well-being, before all of this unreasonable subjecting, pointing fingers at the alienated parent with coordinates from a biased but supported mother, so many organizations, give complete refuge to ladies with complete generosity, ooooh you're a lady, although with a common family, with a rather shadowed upbringing, we adhere to support such corruption.

DON'T TRY TO LET ALL things come to disturb you, as there will come a time when realisation starts to unravel itself, with your nobility and professionalism, staying in control of your mind and thoughts, although it is normal to have these thoughts of hatred and resentment sometimes, more importantly having control of our actions with a stronghold. Always remember the law having been given secondary evidence from reports from your ex-partner, police evidence, but remember these are secondary evidence, not hard-based witnessed evidence. I am just surmising what you could be up against, these are just tests, to see if you are the person responsible for these so-called false allegations. I mean you may have happily left your ex-partner then all of a sudden, these drastic measures and stories have escalated, I am quite sure they have seen and witnessed many similar situations if not thousands.

Let's conclude & summarise Chapter 1,

Before we move onto Chapter 2, we have overseen and overlooked physical well-being and provided you with ideas, that will benefit you have an opportunity to change your circumstances, to live a happier, healthier lifestyle, and also better mental health, with both support through the courts and contact details listed below, how to act in a professional noble mannerism when acting as a correspondent via email to the Court officials, however as above you may find 'Social Services & CaffCass' more of a biased, but more feminist supportive towards mothers. But also, as suggested you can reach out to the NHS, support networks, and for Mental health team, it will pay to make sacrifices from friends who don't consider your wellbeing and mental health as a priority. Leading up to the Courts. As an adult you need to be leading by example, not just for your own sake, but you hold an encompassing encouraging legacy for your children, so make sure you make that a wise one. We have also covered the psychological impact that the mother, keeping the children alienated, away from the father, is rather damaging, we gave examples of the gender roles in both mother and father and the importance that the child doesn't feel left to become interconnectedness, which can lead to self-destruction for the child/teenager growing up, which later will put all the blame to his/her mother or father for their participation in their separation. I would also like you to know I have been aligned at the forefront of the Family Law Judiciary, speaking not only to Judges, Lawyers, and Solicitors but also being involved on a board of studies in a Zoom meeting inside Westminster

Parliament, which is the biggest Judiciary in the United Kingdom, of where they legislate laws, I wanted to raise this awareness, as an issue we all face is 'International bill of rights' egalitarianism. And as any parent, we all deserve equal opportunities, such as children free to speak and express the opinions of their minds, not manipulated by monies, or overpowering corrupting their little minds with unforeseen lies.

Useful contacts Mind's services

- Mind's[1]helpli[2]n[3]e[4]s[5]pro[6]vide information and support by phone and email.

- Local[7]Mi[8]n[9]d[10]s[11]o[12]ff[13]er face-to-face services across England and Wales. These services include talking therapies, peer support and advocacy.

---

1. https://www.mind.org.uk/information-support/helplines/
2. https://www.mind.org.uk/information-support/helplines/
3. https://www.mind.org.uk/information-support/helplines/
4. https://www.mind.org.uk/information-support/helplines/
5. https://www.mind.org.uk/information-support/helplines/
6. https://www.mind.org.uk/information-support/helplines/
7. https://www.mind.org.uk/about-us/local-minds/
8. https://www.mind.org.uk/about-us/local-minds/
9. https://www.mind.org.uk/about-us/local-minds/
10. https://www.mind.org.uk/about-us/local-minds/
11. https://www.mind.org.uk/about-us/local-minds/
12. https://www.mind.org.uk/about-us/local-minds/
13. https://www.mind.org.uk/about-us/local-minds/

- Side by S[14]i[15]d[16]e[17]is[18]our supportive online community for anyone experiencing a mental health problem.

Other organisations

Anxiety UK

Advice and support for people living with anxiety Beat

British Association for Counselling and Psychotherapy (BACP)bacp.co[19].[20]u[21]k[22]Professional body for talking therapy and counselling. Provides information and a list of accredited therapists.

---

14. https://www.mind.org.uk/information-support/side-by-side-our-online-community/
15. https://www.mind.org.uk/information-support/side-by-side-our-online-community/
16. https://www.mind.org.uk/information-support/side-by-side-our-online-community/
17. https://www.mind.org.uk/information-support/side-by-side-our-online-community/
18. https://www.mind.org.uk/information-support/side-by-side-our-online-community/
19. https://www.bacp.co.uk/
20. https://www.bacp.co.uk/
21. https://www.bacp.co.uk/
22. https://www.bacp.co.uk/

Campaign Against Living Miserably (CALM) Provides listening services, information, and support for anyone who needs to talk, including a web chat.

Carers UK

0808 808 7777

029 2081 1370 (Carers Wales)

Advice and support for anyone who provides care.

Information and support for people living with a disability.

FRANK

Confidential advice and information about drugs, their effects, and the law.

Information and support for people affected by mental health problems in Wales.

Hearing Voices Networkhear[23]i[24]ngvoices.[25]o[26]r[27]g[28]Information

23. http://www.hearing-voices.org/

24. http://www.hearing-voices.org/

25. http://www.hearing-voices.org/

26. http://www.hearing-voices.org/

and support for people who hear voices or have other unshared perceptions, including local support groups.

Mental health service run by and for LGBTQ+ people.

National Institute for Health and Care

Excellence (NICE)nice.org[29].[30]u[31]k[32]

Produces guidelines on best practice in healthcare.

Information about health problems and treatments, including details of local NHS services in England.

No Panic

Provides a helpline, step-by-step programmes, and support for people with anxiety disorders.

Papyrus HOPELINEUK

Freepost SAMARITANS LETTERS samaritans.[33]o[34]r[35]g[36]

---

27. http://www.hearing-voices.org/

28. http://www.hearing-voices.org/

29. https://www.nice.org.uk/

30. https://www.nice.org.uk/

31. https://www.nice.org.uk/

32. https://www.nice.org.uk/

33. https://www.samaritans.org/

Samaritans are open 24/7 for anyone who needs to talk. You can visit some Samaritans[37]branch[38]e[39]s[40]i[41]n[42]per[43]s[44]o[45]n[46].[47]Sa[4]
[8]maritans also have a Welsh Language Line on 0808 164 0123 (7pm–11pm every day).

Offers emotional support and information for anyone affected by mental health problems. Mental health charity that supports students.

Time to

Changet[49]i[50]m[51]e[52]-[53]t[54]o[55]change.org[56].[57]u[58]k[59] ([60]E[61]ngland)

---

34. https://www.samaritans.org/
35. https://www.samaritans.org/
36. https://www.samaritans.org/
37. https://www.samaritans.org/branches
38. https://www.samaritans.org/branches
39. https://www.samaritans.org/branches
40. https://www.samaritans.org/branches
41. https://www.samaritans.org/branches
42. https://www.samaritans.org/branches
43. https://www.samaritans.org/branches
44. https://www.samaritans.org/branches
45. https://www.samaritans.org/branches
46. https://www.samaritans.org/branches
47. https://www.samaritans.org/branches
48. https://www.samaritans.org/branches
49. https://www.time-to-change.org.uk/
50. https://www.time-to-change.org.uk/

timetochan[62]g[63]ewales.org.[64]u[65]k[66]([67]Wa[68]les) National campaign to end stigma and discrimination against people with mental health problems in England and Wales. The campaign for England ended in 2021, but its resources are still available point.co[69].[70]u[71]k[72]

---

51. https://www.time-to-change.org.uk/
52. https://www.time-to-change.org.uk/
53. https://www.time-to-change.org.uk/
54. https://www.time-to-change.org.uk/
55. https://www.time-to-change.org.uk/
56. https://www.time-to-change.org.uk/
57. https://www.time-to-change.org.uk/
58. https://www.time-to-change.org.uk/
59. https://www.time-to-change.org.uk/
60. https://www.time-to-change.org.uk/
61. https://www.time-to-change.org.uk/
62. https://www.timetochangewales.org.uk/
63. https://www.timetochangewales.org.uk/
64. https://www.timetochangewales.org.uk/
65. https://www.timetochangewales.org.uk/
66. https://www.timetochangewales.org.uk/
67. https://www.timetochangewales.org.uk/
68. https://www.timetochangewales.org.uk/
69. https://www.turning-point.co.uk/
70. https://www.turning-point.co.uk/
71. https://www.turning-point.co.uk/
72. https://www.turning-point.co.uk/

Health and social care services in England for people with a learning disability. Also supports people with mental health problems, drug and alcohol abuse or unemployment.

YoungMinds

0808 802 5544 (Parents Helpline)

85258 (Crisis Messenger for young people – text the letters YM)youngminds.org[73].[74]u[75]k[76]Committed to improving the mental health of babies, children, and young people,

- Call 116 123 to talk toSamarita[77]n[78]s[79],[80]o[81]r

jo@samaritans.orgem ail:

- hours
- Text "SHOUT" to 85258 to contact the
- Shout Crisis Text Li[82]n[83]e[84],[85]o[86]r text "YM" if you're under 19

---

73. https://www.youngminds.org.uk/
74. https://www.youngminds.org.uk/
75. https://www.youngminds.org.uk/
76. https://www.youngminds.org.uk/
77. https://www.samaritans.org/how-we-can-help/contact-samaritan/
78. https://www.samaritans.org/how-we-can-help/contact-samaritan/
79. https://www.samaritans.org/how-we-can-help/contact-samaritan/
80. https://www.samaritans.org/how-we-can-help/contact-samaritan/
81. https://www.samaritans.org/how-we-can-help/contact-samaritan/

including

Support for parents and carers.

If you just need to talk, any time of day or night.

Free listening services

on If you're under 19, you can also call 0800 1111 to talk toChildli[87]n[88]e[89].[90]T[91]he number will not appear on your phone bill.

SERVICES OFFER CONFIDENTIAL support from trained volunteers. You can talk about anything that's troubling you, no matter how difficult:

> Make sure you plan to try and better your Mental Health & Well-being, remember plenty of sleep, stay hydrated not intoxicated, exercise minimal

82. https://www.giveusashout.org/
83. https://www.giveusashout.org/
84. https://www.giveusashout.org/
85. https://www.giveusashout.org/
86. https://www.giveusashout.org/
87. https://www.childline.org.uk/
88. https://www.childline.org.uk/
89. https://www.childline.org.uk/
90. https://www.childline.org.uk/
91. https://www.childline.org.uk/

2hours per week and eat well remembering your 5 a day.

The eat-well plate gives you some idea what your plate should consist of, remembering average calories intake is roughly 2500 on the average person.

Chapter ii

As you have witnessed through the previous chapter, it really takes perseverance and knowing the right route and avenues that will help you in advance to you and your child/children. Which you may seem fair or unfair, maybe a lesson of lawlessness. I really hope you don't feel this as strolling on without direction information sources. Because easy direct information doesn't come so easily, as we suggested before a solicitor can charge from anything around £250 an hour, there are a list of local McKenzie friends who can act on your behalf, most of which want paying also, some less expensive than others. McKenzie friend who are they? They act on your behalf through any Family Court trial, and up and coming hearings, they may not be allowed to speak on your behalf but most certainly help prepare questions and court letters, Where they can be found (McKenzie Friend) it's worth doing a google or engine web search online at your nearest, local constituency McKenzie friend branch (Essex McKenzie Friend, 2023), some not all can be so much cheaper than a solicitor with their fees to act as a correspondents to the Court officials, having already dealt with years of experienced cases, if you possibly know a friend of a friend to a McKenzie friend which in that case, could work out better for you, having said that your friend can reference you being father figure to your offspring, The Mckenzie friend will act on your behalf through the family court hearing, directing the presumption against you rebuttable.

<u>Before applying to the family Courts:</u>

There are many steps you need to take before applying to the court, firstly considering, either a solicitor or McKenzie friend to act as your correspondent, now it's time to evaluate your situation, separation between you your exspouse/relationship and offspring, was it a separation/break-up which left on amicable terms? If not it's okay not many relationships left on good terms, we learn that through human errors and what's broken can't be fixed majority of the time. If you think you may be able to get someone to act on your behalf to liaison with your ex-partner, having said that she can be fairly reasonable, it will be worth contacting your local/constituency mediation contact centre, they can either provide you with support to be in further contact with your ex-partner, and mediate between you and her about the relationship with you and the children and quite possibly having some planned contact to start, but many cases leave very undoubtedly. But if you don't ask the answer is always going to be a no.(© 2023 Family Mediation Council, 2023) The mediation centres are provided by your local council and a Government recognisable Organisation, they will ask you to attend their centre, to take some legal and personal I.D. one of their assistance will provide you with support after filling out their documents, then they will discuss your options moving forward, are you on the birth certificate or not, are you the biological parent, this will indicate whether you will need a C100 or a C1 form, you need the mediation to sign the first court papers, that presents the reasons why mediation isn't going to be amicable or accessible between you and your expartner/spouse, if you are out of work and currently on benefit income you'll be eligible for help with court fees. (Court fees, 2023) you can access all the information online, I have used indented citations and references at the back of the Booklet, to help you find the information source accurately. The overall discipline of a mediator as follows and what they can provide in the realms of support.

What is family mediation?

Family mediation is a process in which an independent, professionally trained mediator helps you find agreements regarding your children and finances after separation.

Mediation can also be helpful when arrangements you have previously made need to

be changed, especially as your children grow older.

Mediation helps you keep control. No one forces you to do anything against your will. The mediator will help you find a solution that works for both of you and explain what needs to happen for your agreement to be legally binding.

FMC approved mediators have helped hundreds of thousands of families agree on post-separation financial arrangements and find collaborative parenting post-separation.

This process is much less stressful and quicker than going to court and can save you money. Legal assistance is available if you qualify financially. Mediators work with separating couples in a flexible way to suit your circumstances. You don't have to be in the same space as your ex if you or your mediator decides that it would be better to work with you in separate spaces. Your more than likely feeling anxious with such a prolonged preparation to try and make contact with your offspring, just remember taking the first steps is better than most fathers, who we initially seeing on a day-to-day basis mothers saying their baby father is a deadbeat. No doubt your offspring is already poisoned by mothers care that your deadbeat regardless as it tends to be the general norm in the midst of any separation, if you position simple as easy, which we both know and are fully aware nothing is either just simple or easy. Just know that you're not the only one up against alienation/separation from your offspring, its somewhat heartbreaking/ heart wrenching to know the lengths we have to go to, just to show you are a caring responsible father. I mean was the separation due to the lack of money, made redundant perhaps, does money justify stability over responsibility? What money cannot buy is responsibility, money to some senses can buy stability, questionable the stability of the person using the money, what for? Fun filled days out for the family as a whole, booze cruises abroad, children swinging of the rafters of the boat perhaps, the mind matters, so if the person with the money is not prioritizing the children first, then their mental health & wellbeing is now in subjected to be questioned. I strongly believe that stability doesn't necessarily have to be based on the foundation of money, but more importantly here in the U.K., the care, encouragement and compassion, integrity and direction one can provide for their offspring, and ultimately giving guidance and a freedom to choose and speech so that the offspring is imbalance for a perfect opportunity and upbringing. But not forgetting to look further than your nose to find the nearest ***Family Law Mediators*** (Family Law, 2023) within you're your local constituency, but please also bare in mind they may not be able to help you, if your ex-spouse and offsprings have moved away from your district. Although it seems to become a problem in many cases, but we can only assume not every case has been similar and we don't know if we don't try. But I am sure your determination will expand to do whatever it takes, and if that means chasing them around the Countryside, you'll find their nearest family mediation centre and start to make enquiries there. But there is nothing wrong with making your queries either by telephone contact or email, they'll also have a website which will provide you with a list of options, such as divorce & separation, as no separation has become easy from your offsprings, financial settlements, resolving the issues that you may or may have not yet settled between you and your ex-partner, as most men just tend to walk and leave everything for their children, they also support unmarried couples & domestic abuse disputes, word of advice it is best to try and get everything out in the open and off your chest, as mediation are there to help guide you through the first part of finding your nearest family Judiciary, and this will further indicate the theological process to getting your Court proceedings moving forward, it may take several months before you receive any email from the Family Law Court proceedings, just to indicate you that they have received the mediation documents, but your assistant at the mediation centre will also explain how long the process really is, with so many back-logs running through the Courts, many people are those who have been awaiting a year to get the hearing into the Courts, so it's best to not have any high expectations, you or anyone else doesn't have a higher or lower priority than the other. But just know this, you had the enthusiasm, encouragement to keep fighting. Be ever so proud of yourself that you have come this far, alienated parents struggle, of putting up, the good fight. for their own right and their own children. If you feel at any moment you think it's necessary to give up on those children then you have been defeated by a losing battle, you are the alienated parent, become alienated to those children also, you and them alike are both suffering the consequences from the breakdown of relationship, you personally own this responsibility to them, don't become the deadbeat parent you've been called out to be, like many other alienated parents, just giving up hope. You'd be neglecting them and making it easy for the system to justly agree. The injustice and lawlessness that goes on is a very weak system but without hope & perseverance, you'll will never be able to strengthen and beat the system, I said previously they consider bribery, siding with the majority rather than quality, when I say quality, doesn't mean like a label to nobility, hierarchy, it means a compassionate, loving, caring, parent. So let's take this into account, use your perseverance you need that fire motivation in your heart, fuel that fire with determination, because these are your children being failed by the system of things, by no negligence of your own, but due to breakdown of relationship, we are going to put that part behind us, as that hadn't worked out, your resilience is what you need to thrive with, all the ammunition what comes ahead and what lies before you, quarrelling, accusations of abuse, this that and the other, without primary evidence, cancel it out! I mean they may or may have not some sort of evidence, but me and you both know only our consciousness knows what relevant and what's irrelevant. 'All this talk she was an angel in heaven. She is a beast, here too, on earth'! You probably question yourself whose accountability to yours and your children's psychological damage being separated so long, you missed out on birthdays, holidays, Christmas days, the kids sports days, school plays, graduation days and parent evenings, all these activities the love, caring, compassionate, encouragement that every single child wants is that thanks giving their father can give and be proud!

With progressive, progression that slowly awaits, through the all that dreaded ambitions, anxiety's, torments, knowing that we still have those dreaded proceedings to face, you have proven that you are an honourable parent, for the fact that you are still improvising through the system of things..

(Several Months later)

You should've had a response back, received an email from your local Family Court, within that response back from the Court, as addressed, dated to you, make sure you **save** the recipients email in your address book as this will be your correspondent email address, also at the top left of the email you'll see the **title subject area, this will have your Court Case Reference Number:** At this stage I hope you've prioritized the importance of filing, it may be worth buying a note pad, which labels important court documentation. Within the recipients Court Letter, should be stated how the proceedings will start to build a case, please note that, in every response back to the Courts, it will not only pay, but also good practice as any correspondent would agree, upon your name, home address, post-code, contact details and dated. And again, not forgetting your reference number in the Subject area, whilst the courts start to build the case, in which usually are fact findings, many factors they will want to find out. Before making an application, the welfare of your child/children's Mental health and wellbeing, such as CaffCass reports and Social Services reports, who are they, CaffCas? And what they stand for? Children and Family Court Advisory and

Support Service, they will be in contact individually by email, possibly with a list of questions to be answered similar to the Court letter, your role to the Children, are you on the birth certificate, your child/children's D.O.B. The CaffCass will want to contact you, to arrange a general meeting at your address. To familiarise themselves with your hopes and appraisals moving forward, remembering they are on the understanding of a breakdown in the relationship between you and your ex-spouse, so just be on the lookout and awareness of questions that will be asked, as they know your ex-spouses will be making counter claims against you trying to make any contact with your offsprings, it's really not worth trying to start speaking about how bad your ex partner was, as your main interest at this point and focus is your offsprings, visualise the importance of you being involved in your child/children's life, speak to them in how you would like to build your relationship back with your children, and what are the best steps to take moving forward, it will be worth saying that you as a loving parent care about your child/childrens well-being and their safety which is paramount, it may be worth saying if you know or don't know that your ex-spouse may have moved in another partner with her and your offsprings, as this will alert them to make safety checks, and quite possibly alert the courts, to ask for a children's protection order, with that deemed as necessary. Whilst having alerted a CaffCass worker they would have filed your concerns and raised with awareness to the Courts about your child/childrens safety, The Judge would consider your wishes, and more than likely pursue a section 37 report be carried out, which normally takes effect to Social Services, firstly what is a section 37 report? (2023, 2023) the court has the power to order an investigation by alocal authority[1] into the welfare

of a child if it appears that a public law order, namely asupervision order[2] or acare order,[3] may be appropriate. The investigation will result in a report, often referred to as a 'section 37 report', as previously suggested the Court would then pursue local authority to investigate the welfare of your child/children, with that being said, (Social Services) would be that local authority. They would be attending your ex partners address. But also like we have suggested in chapter one, it's rather peculiar, that they don't find neutral terms to face the children in such a crisis, facing both parent and child/children alienation. I mean the importance of the psychological separation needs to be met on civil grounds, to let the child/children be able to voice their freedom to rights and speech.

---

1. https://www.lexisnexis.co.uk/legal/glossary/local-authority

2. https://www.lexisnexis.co.uk/legal/glossary/supervision-order-

3. https://www.lexisnexis.co.uk/legal/glossary/care-order

THE COMMON GENERALIZATION and visualization

Coming through the system of things, as your mind starts to ponder into the drift of the midst of things, which is a norm an anxiously awaits your first initial Court hearing date, with my guidance and preparation to what could or may not possibly what lies ahead, but also very likely similar the normal behaviours around the build up to finalize this long awaited Family Court hearing, with its common interests involving all parties, you may or not face your opposing Ex Spouse, with feelings that have left her daunted, this is the generalization, amid of her coercive control that she deems it necessary to stop yours and her child/children having any contact with you. They will go to many lengths, just through pure guilt, and much resentment to not make any appearances through the court system. You may have already started to reason this, if she had already made a Non-Molestation order against you. This is the guilt not pleasing of the children, but rather a guilt that it pleasing to herself. Many times, in these situations, Social Services, and CaffCass would've already, also been manipulated by her narcissistic brutality of coercive endeavouring repulsive lies. This doesn't leave you with a positive standing point moving forward through the Court Process, but what I will suggest is that you don't start playing the same game as your ex-spouse, tarnishing one another. Your resilience and endurance are all that you need, your resilience to stay calm, your resilience to only encompass your fathering responsibilities to your child/children. And what benefits them by showing what love and encouragement can do as a father to your child/children. It is rather vital that any biological father is apparent around his child/children's upbringings, as it has physiological support and guidance to their mentality, many Psychologists and psychiatrists argue the importance having a close bond with both parents can influence and guide their children, but without that close relationship can cause human errors of feeling of interconnectedness, which can drive the child/children, to lack of enthusiasm, low-selfesteem, turning to unsociable behaviour, constant being attacked by bullying, many acts of lawlessness can compromise within your child/children future, if you don't start to address your concerns of your child's welfare having hope that you are outlining the key importance to your role as a father. So now you can get a perfect picture to what it's meant, by the term ***Generalization & Visualization,*** very correlated with a premeditated assumption *to try and alter your direction to having any form of contact with your children, it makes you start to question of whom is giving these directional tactics to your ex-spouse to counter-act your appeal to the children? Is it Social Services, CaffCass. I mean who is giving her these tactics, of knowing full well not to turn up to the Family Court throughout the hearing's regards to your child/children, which are meaningful tactics to prolong such case. Remembering not each case are the same, and many ex-spouses act totally different accordingly. You may find some expartners will proact through the Court order, through the anxiousness and feelings of a guilty consciousness towards you and your children, with hope that this is your case as it may help things additionally quicker through The Family Courts Proceedings and hopeful contact to start sooner, rather than later! When you overlook the punitive psychological aspects that you have been dealt with, you probably* *have already foreseen metaphorical transition through the biological correspondent through Mother, like daughter , symptoms, maybe you would've picked up on this already overlooking your spouse's siblings with different father's, which will answer your traditional query about this unsubscribed outraged punitive treatment you, and your offsprings are facing. But contrary to this you cannot outreach the blame through bad conduct of upbringing through the Nan/grandmother's perspective of things, but rather raise this awareness prior to the trial within the Family Court proceedings, Social Services, CaffCass and any other organisation with all hope that someone somewhere shall support you within such irregular circumstances.*

What is Parent Alienation?

At the most basic level, parental alienation refers to the process by which a child becomes irrationally attached to one parent and expresses hatred or rejection of the other in a fight or flight- separated! This is often due to behaviours that the consensual parent exhibits that manipulate the child's beliefs and perceptions of the alienated parent, as well as the distortion or erasure of any positive memories that the child has. Having said of which may or may not be about that.

Now thinking back, with mediations advice, and discussions which will be raised to the awareness of any financial settlements to be arranged, i.e. mortgages property with value, Under the Court's Jurisdiction and Section 38 if they deem advisable or necessary,

Court Jurisdiction and Venue

Section 38 of the Family Law Act 1996 concerns the jurisdiction of the court and venue. The Circuit Court having jurisdiction to hear and determine proceedings under this Act and in connection with which that jurisdiction is concerned is called the Circuit Family Court1. Section 38(1) also clearly states that cohabitants and former cohabitants do not have the right to occupy the same residential house in which they live or have lived together2. Under sections 33 and 35 to 38 of the Family Law Act 1996, the court has the power to make a protection order known as an occupation order3.

38Neither cohabitant or former cohabitant entitled to occupy.

(1)This section applies if—

(a)one cohabitant or former cohabitant and the other cohabitant or former cohabitant occupy a dwelling-house which is the home in which they [[4]**F1**[5]c[6]ohabit or cohabited]; but

(b)neither of them is entitled to remain in occupation—

(i)by virtue of a beneficial estate or interest or contract; or

---

4. https://www.legislation.gov.uk/ukpga/1996/27/section/38#commentary-c20993651

5. https://www.legislation.gov.uk/ukpga/1996/27/section/38#commentary-c20993651

6. https://www.legislation.gov.uk/ukpga/1996/27/section/38#commentary-c20993651

(ii)by virtue of any enactment giving him the right to remain in occupation.

(2)Either of the parties may apply to the court for an order against the other under this section. (3)An order under this section may—

(a)require the respondent to permit the applicant to enter and remain in the dwellinghouse or part of the dwelling-house;

(b)regulate the occupation of the dwelling-house by either or both of the parties;

(c)require the respondent to leave the dwellinghouse or part of the dwelling-house; or

(d)exclude the respondent from a defined area in which the dwelling-house is included.

(4)In deciding whether to exercise its powers to include one or more of the provisions referred to in subsection (3) ("a subsection (3) provision") and (if so) in what manner, the court shall have regard to all the circumstances including—

(a)the housing needs and housing resources of each of the parties and of any relevant child; (b)the financial resources of each of the parties;

(c)the likely effect of any order, or of any decision by the court not to exercise its powers under subsection (3), on the health, safety or well-being of the parties and of any relevant child;

(d)the conduct of the parties in relation to each other and otherwise; and

(e)the questions mentioned in subsection (5).

(5)The questions are—

(a)whether the applicant or any relevant child is likely to suffer significant harm attributable to conduct of the respondent if the subsection (3) provision is not included in the order; and

(b)whether the harm likely to be suffered by the respondent or child if the provision is included is as great as or greater than the harm attributable to conduct of the respondent which is likely to be suffered by the applicant or child if the provision is not included.

(6)An order under this section shall be limited so as to have effect for a specified period not exceeding six months, but may be extended on one occasion for a further specified period not exceeding six months. (Crown & database, 2023)

This will determine a financial agreement between, the Judge, you, your ex-spouse and offspring/offsprings. And what is deemed necessary to all your welfare and wellbeing's combined. However, through every family dispute and breakdown through marriage it will become justifiable through The Family Courts to discover what is feasible and necessary and to provide a deficit, through house valuation or businesses that you had throughout the marriage. And upon separation dividing it between, yourself, spouse and offsprings. Whilst overlooking each individual's welfare & wellbeing, making sure the disparity of monies in separation is within response of the individuals basic circumstances.

Let's further our understanding of both Court process, procedures and what can possibly concur during a relationship break-up, breakdown, which is the general norm in today's modern society of things. Although it is not the best practice moving forward for your child/children to also suffer the consequences of alienation, as months, years have drifted apart, you will begin to wonder your child/children's welfare and wellbeing. It is normal for us inhabitants both male & female alike, to find affection, a partner to share emotions and compassion again with, but having said that, what you don't want now as the separated father, is the stepfather, to be acting inappropriately to your ex-spouse in front of your children. Even more admittedly when you haven't been allowed any contact. with your offsprings, what you don't want is your child/children is to start emulating the nuances of their stepfather, which could be encouraging your child/children's future into the completely opposite direction. I genuinely mean nobody should be choosing their child/children's future, they should let them decide their own options, but without the influence of either opposing party. For they could end up choosing unwise option, that grasps hold of a shift pattern that has a downward spiral, causing conflict or possible isolation/ imprisonment. With biological father and mothers support with both knowing the welfare of their child/children, they would require, what is feasible and applicable to their child's/ children's wellbeing having their best interests & circumstances at heart, as they both would know what would benefit them with their current health related tasks and educational needs that they would require for their future goals and gains to be applicable in their field of knowledge.

Having already spoken with your local mediation centre it may be worth suggesting your concerns around all the key areas that focuses on what you could possibly think that could determine your child's/children's future. If they oppose this, they may order a section 7, **What will a Section 7 Report contain?**

A Section 7 report must contain all relevant background information in relation to the parents and the child, key facts, and evidence that the needs of the child have been considered in accordance with the Welfare Checklist. The report will also consider the child's wishes and feelings, dependent upon their age and whether they are able to express these clearly, and what the author of the report considers to be in the best interests of the child.

The welfare of the child will always be the Court's paramount (most important) consideration.

The person who prepares the report may speak to the child (depending on their age and understanding) about their wishes and feelings and what they would like to happen. They will also spend time with both parties and listen to any concerns they may have. They may also speak to other people such as family members, teachers, and health workers. They will not ask the child to decide or to choose between the parents as to who they should live with and any contact they will have with the non-resident parent.

If it appears to the court that the applicant or any relevant child is likely to suffer significant harm attributable to conduct of the respondent if an order under this section containing one or more of the provisions mentioned in subsection (3) is not made, the court shall make the order unless it appears to it that—

(a)the respondent or any relevant child is likely to suffer significant harm if the order is made; and

(b)the harm likely to be suffered by the respondent or child in that event is as great as, or greater than, the harm attributable to conduct of the respondent which is likely to be suffered by the applicant or child if the order is not made.

(Astills, 2023)

What is the Welfare Checklist?

When deciding matters

When deciding matters in respect of the children, a Court needs to take into account the welfare checklist:

a. the ascertainable wishes and feeling of the child concerned (considered in the light of the child's age and understanding);
b. the child's physical, emotional and educational needs;
c. the likely effect on the child of any change in his/her circumstances;
d. the child's age, sex, background, and any other characteristic which the court considers relevant;

e. any harm which the child has suffered or is at risk of suffering;
f. how capable each of the child's parents, and any other person in relation to whom the court considers the question to be relevant, is of meeting the child's needs;
g. the range of powers available to the court under the Children Act in the proceedings in question.

I'm not happy with the Section 7 report, what can I do?

If you do not agree with the report it is important that you let the Court know your concerns, including in relation to what you consider to be any factual inaccuracies in the report and any disagreement you have in respect of the recommendations contained within the report. The judge will consider your concerns when making a decision.

Who makes the final decision?

After reading the report and listening to what you and other people in the case have said, the Court will make the final decision about what should happen to your children, if an agreement cannot be reached between parents. The Court will make the decision based on what is best for the child. It will take into account their wishes and feelings, but the order may not be in accordance with the child's wishes and feelings if this is not considered to be in their best interests. The decision will be set out in a Court Order which you must comply with.

Important psychological facts!

But as I were suggesting previously to determine any child/children's best interest's, feeling's, emotions and best wishes, you'll never get a civil honest response if asked these such questions without being asked from the opposed parent who is both alienating the other, children and supposedly father away from one another, because children response will be based from the inner fear from their mother which would already tried her upmost respect to poison and manipulate the child/children's teleological response to direct them away from the truth, but should become reasonable within the terms to the matter, to find an encompassing but encouraging designated area which is more on neutral grounds away from any unreasonable witnesses to let your child/children have a freedom of speech, to find out the truth with regards to their best interest and wishes.

After analysing section 7 report:

The judge, CaffCass & the Social worker would've analysed the child/children's interest's and best wishes moving forward, which they would then consider how to make things in aligned with child/children arrangement order. You will be asked, these questions prior to the court proceedings, by either CaffCass or Social Services, which they would scrivere within their reports to the Judge and any other Court official that is deemed applicable upon the Court hearing, of what your best wishes and interest are facing a child arrangement order, it will be worth to consider some form of contact to build the necessary steps back into your child/children's life, even if it means writing a simple letter or preferably contact via phone call, then prior to building your relationship back together with these small steps, the next action's to take would be for the benefit of you and your child's/children's welfare, mental health & wellbeing is to ask to have contact to start within a counselling arrangement, which shows you are willing to comply with directed professional support. When you can proact with the system of things this can generate more possible leads to having overnight stays, then you could go back to the Court and then arrange ultimate weekends, birthdays, Christmas holidays, half term and summer holidays, maybe come to a conclusion of things and have joint priority to school run's and sport days, school play's and parent's evening's and this may advance you to be able to attend school trips with your child/children. Metaphorically speaking in the term of historical and the cultural educational influence that they deem as necessary support to that child/children in subject of course, with that reason alone would seem the necessary steps to take to advance your child's/children's learning, throughout the support and encouraging guidance that one can give. Which hypothetically speaking it's an opportunity that nobody else can give. However, it all boils down to the judge's consideration and reports that have been passed on through social workers and CaffCass.

The child arrangement order section 8 in question, as follows

: 8[F1[7]C[8]hild arrangements orders] and other orders with respect to children.

---

7. https://www.legislation.gov.uk/ukpga/1989/41/section/8#commentary-key-1db7642033b04017fe5541d21d35f1c3
8. https://www.legislation.gov.uk/ukpga/1989/41/section/8#commentary-key-1db7642033b04017fe5541d21d35f1c3

(1)In this Act —

- "[[9]**F2**[10]c[11]hild arrangements order" means an order regulating arrangements relating to any of the following—

(a)

with whom a child is to live, spend time or otherwise have contact, and

(b)

when a child is to live, spend time or otherwise have contact with any person;]

- **F3**[12].[13]..

- "a prohibited steps order" means an order that no step which could be taken by a parent in meeting his parental responsibility for a child, and which is of

---

9. https://www.legislation.gov.uk/ukpga/1989/41/section/8#commentary-key-55c87fa018ade0afbfaca94717757c90
10. https://www.legislation.gov.uk/ukpga/1989/41/section/8#commentary-key-55c87fa018ade0afbfaca94717757c90
11. https://www.legislation.gov.uk/ukpga/1989/41/section/8#commentary-key-55c87fa018ade0afbfaca94717757c90
12. https://www.legislation.gov.uk/ukpga/1989/41/section/8#commentary-key-3a37c0eddeaa16e78d50a5126f83ceb8
13. https://www.legislation.gov.uk/ukpga/1989/41/section/8#commentary-key-3a37c0eddeaa16e78d50a5126f83ceb8

a kind specified in the order, shall be taken by any person without the consent of the court;

- **F3**[14] .[15]..

- "a specific issue order" means an order giving directions for the purpose of determining a specific question which has arisen, or which may arise, in connection with any aspect of parental responsibility for a child.

(2)In this Act "a section 8 order" means any of the orders mentioned in subsection (1) and any order varying or discharging such an order.

(3)For the purposes of this Act "family proceedings" means any proceedings—

(a)under the inherent jurisdiction of the High Court in relation to children; and

(b)under the enactments mentioned in subsection (4),

but does not include proceedings on an application for leave under section 100(3).

(4)The enactments are—

(a)Parts I, II and IV of this Act;

---

14. https://www.legislation.gov.uk/ukpga/1989/41/section/8#commentary-key-3a37c0eddeaa16e78d50a5126f83ceb8

15. https://www.legislation.gov.uk/ukpga/1989/41/section/8#commentary-key-3a37c0eddeaa16e78d50a5126f83ceb8

(b)the**M1**[16]M[17]atrimonial Causes Act 1973;

[[18]**F4**[19]([20]ba)Schedule 5 to the Civil Partnership Act 2004;]

[[21]**F5**[22]([23]c)the**M2**[24]Domestic Violence and Matrimonial

Proceedings Act 1976;

(d)the Adoption and Children Act 2002;]

(e)the**M3**[25]D[26]omestic Proceedings and Magistrates' Courts Act 1978;

[[27]**F6**[28]([29]ea)Schedule 6 to the Civil Partnership Act 2004;]

---

16. https://www.legislation.gov.uk/ukpga/1989/41/section/8#commentary-c15159671

17. https://www.legislation.gov.uk/ukpga/1989/41/section/8#commentary-c15159671

18. https://www.legislation.gov.uk/ukpga/1989/41/section/8#commentary-c18773541

19. https://www.legislation.gov.uk/ukpga/1989/41/section/8#commentary-c18773541

20. https://www.legislation.gov.uk/ukpga/1989/41/section/8#commentary-c18773541

21. https://www.legislation.gov.uk/ukpga/1989/41/section/8#commentary-c15159681

22. https://www.legislation.gov.uk/ukpga/1989/41/section/8#commentary-c15159681

23. https://www.legislation.gov.uk/ukpga/1989/41/section/8#commentary-c15159681

24. https://www.legislation.gov.uk/ukpga/1989/41/section/8#commentary-c15159691

25. https://www.legislation.gov.uk/ukpga/1989/41/section/8#commentary-c15159711

26. https://www.legislation.gov.uk/ukpga/1989/41/section/8#commentary-c15159711

[[30]**F5**[31]([32]f)sections 1 and 9 of the**M4**[33]Matrimonial Homes Act 1983;]

(g)Part III of the**M5**[34]M[35]atrimonial and Family Proceedings Act 1984.

F7[36][(h)the Family Law Act 1996]

[[37]**F8**[38]([39]i)sections 11 and 12 of the Crime and Disorder Act 1998.]

---

27. **https://www.legislation.gov.uk/ukpga/1989/41/section/8#commentary-c18773561**
28. **https://www.legislation.gov.uk/ukpga/1989/41/section/8#commentary-c18773561**
29. https://www.legislation.gov.uk/ukpga/1989/41/section/8#commentary-c18773561
30. **https://www.legislation.gov.uk/ukpga/1989/41/section/8#commentary-c15159681**
31. **https://www.legislation.gov.uk/ukpga/1989/41/section/8#commentary-c15159681**
32. https://www.legislation.gov.uk/ukpga/1989/41/section/8#commentary-c15159681
33. **https://www.legislation.gov.uk/ukpga/1989/41/section/8#commentary-c15159731**
34. **https://www.legislation.gov.uk/ukpga/1989/41/section/8#commentary-c15159741**
35. https://www.legislation.gov.uk/ukpga/1989/41/section/8#commentary-c15159741
36. **https://www.legislation.gov.uk/ukpga/1989/41/section/8#commentary-c15159751**
37. **https://www.legislation.gov.uk/ukpga/1989/41/section/8#commentary-c15159761**
38. **https://www.legislation.gov.uk/ukpga/1989/41/section/8#commentary-c15159761**

[[40]**F9**[41]([42]j)Part 1 of Schedule 2 to the Female Genital Mutilation Act 2003 (other than paragraph 3 of that Schedule).] (Astills, 2023, p. 7)

39. https://www.legislation.gov.uk/ukpga/1989/41/section/8#commentary-c15159761

40. https://www.legislation.gov.uk/ukpga/1989/41/section/8#commentary-key-4d59d76b099c2577a316acd331b495cd

41. https://www.legislation.gov.uk/ukpga/1989/41/section/8#commentary-key-4d59d76b099c2577a316acd331b495cd

42. https://www.legislation.gov.uk/ukpga/1989/41/section/8#commentary-key-4d59d76b099c2577a316acd331b495cd

Knowing the importance within the system can and will be unjust:

With realising what you are up against you would've discovered by now, that it doesn't come easily. With all within accord, the welfare, mental health & wellbeing from all parties, your children, ex-spouse and yourself, you would've thought by now, and worked out a mutual agreement, between the separation and the importance of you being the loving, caring, supportive parent just as they are. But for unforeseen circumstances the bittersweet and twisted other organisations have fallen whilst they swander around amid the drift through the manipulation from your ex-spouse. Social Services & CaffCass which primarily are driven and run by females, tend to negotiate due to the care of children, rather than morally trying talk about the importance of both parents having their dual responsibilities, as mother and father, both the traits and characteristics of both one not like that of the other. If you become either unsatisfied with Social worker or CaffCass worker's you can reason why to the judge and to the Family Court system prior to your court hearing date, by email, or even raise your concern's via the organisations website link, CaffCass or Social Services. If you are finding a difficulty, it's best to contact their service centres and ask for guidance in how to make a complaint as you are not happy with the services they are providing.

We have found an alienated mother's support page, that support alienated mother's, psychological disparity and wellbeing! I am somewhat happy to show that I am impartial, I were narrating the parent Alienation from a male perspective at the time, then halfway through I began to think more broadly about my options, as I have several girlfriends I have become close associates on the drift through alienation myself then to realise it's not just fathers who face segregation away from their offsprings. I feel for anyone who is having experiences, has gone through these experiences of whom needs reflection and direction! I know the journey is hard but hopefully throughout this publication has given you an insight, reflection, perception to give you the strength to carry on and achieve your aspirations of your family reconciliation. "For in your heart your kids will always be a part"!

Anyway I have found Mother's for justice, they are offering support, a retreat within Somerset, to help refresh the mind, with plenty of open air, nice views to let you have a solace space to empty your thoughts!

"Alienated Mothers' Retreat - Family Separation Clinic" ('Alienated Mothers Retreat', 2023) ***A list of useful contacts:***

Who are they:

Where can you find them:

What they offer:

- *Families need dads - Both Parents Matter (FNF), founded in 1974, is a UK registered social care charity providing information, advice and support for parents whose relationships with their children are threatened during or after divorce or separation. , or who have been alienated or separated from their children. FNF also advocates for shared parenting, more time*

for children with non-resident parents, and stronger legal action when resident parents defy court orders requiring them to allow their children to maintain a relationship with the other parent. The organization's goal is that children of divorce or separation do not lose the love and care of a parent. (FNF.Org, 2023) *They have a website which I have referenced within the text within citation and at the back of the book, you can also contact them by telephone:* Helpline: 0300 0300

363. **Helpline: 0300 0300 363**

Objectives and purpose

Families Need Dads is a UK registered charity providing information and support to parents, including unmarried parents, of both sexes. FNF is primarily concerned with issues related to maintaining a child's relationship with both parents during and after family breakdown. Founded in 1974, FNF helps thousands of parents each year.

They can provide you with every aspect of guidance facing The Family Court trial, what they can't do is act on your behalf throughout the court's hearing's, they have the most experience having witnessed and heard several parent alienation trials. They will be able to help guide you how to write an initial set up statement in aligned to your case. On their website you will gather some useful links such as get help on their browser link, Court support and local meetings, where you'll find many others in the same situation as yourself. Also, an emotional support extended link within the help guide section. There is also an information link, with tailing off links such as, Child and parent arrangements, separating, child maintenance, new partners and what to tell children. They have also a forum link, which we can assume many other alienated fathers have anxiety and many questions unanswered, they will be sharing their reviews, evaluations, resolutions, and guidance's through their journey alike of your own. And a place to share your story with others that have already faced the same or very similar to yours, so you will probably find a forum would be the best place to meet likeminded, individuals share ideas and move forward positively.

- **There are several organisations that support alienated parents:** However, as I am a gentleman I am only very familiar with both "Families needs Fathers' & 'Fathers need justice'. Father's for Justice are rather parrel comparing to families need fathers, with their ultimate goal is prioritizing parent alienation across United Kingdom.

You will discover both their websites really helpful, with what they champion and campaign. With both sites observing the national statistics within the UK, with single parent's and how many children within the UK without fathers. ('Alienated Mothers Retreat', 2023) ***Fathers need Justice:*** *"An additional 200 children will have endured the inhumane separation of their fathers in clandestine family courts by the end of today."*

Fathers4Justice's founder, Matt O'Connor

To be fatherless is to be profane. Although every kid has the human right to have a father, almost 1 in 3 children in the UK do not have one; that amounts to almost 4 million fatherless children.

HELP US PUT AN END to the government's inhumane and harsh treatment of families.

Very similar to families need fathers, they also have some helpful links with an option write to your local constituency MP, to see if they support the right to equal parenting or not?

Other links also such as, (our campaign)-Fathers rights: Help advice and support our mission-our campaigns-Case studies- Our 10 point blueprint for Family Law- Contact your MP- F4J Visual archive- Missing children.

Contact us:

Media enquiries Contact No: 07788235250

Email: office@fathers-4-justice.org General enquires: Office@father-4-justice.org

Our story- By Matt O'connor, which he has set his visions and reasons to why he has put his compassion, zeal of heart & soul into supporting Fathers 4 justice, as both he and us alike have faced and still facing one of the utmost horrific injustices within the system of lawlessness.

Take action now – has an online forum where you can make a booking with a consultation case worker at a whole lot less rather than forking out a fortune for Solicitor fees.

There are many options that provide free support facing family trials, these organisations are volunteers that help you preparing addition statement letters opposed to the Courts, with answer or arguing the claim against CaffCass & Social Services reports, I found which was rather useful also, "Support through Court" you will find their support workers do not prioritize a normative study like majority of organisations that you have faced previously, making judgement through false allegations that have been proposed to the courts by ex-spouse and social workers, but more of the sense that they work from an empirical study of which frames the importance of you being involved within your offsprings life. You will find their website through support through court, within your local constituency-County, or if you are finding that a struggle to find, please do contact your local family Court and ask them for their contact number or how to find their website as they will be able to provide you with all the information that you require.

('Support through Family Court', 2023) *What they stand for and what support they have to offer: Standing in Chelmsford court without a lawyer?*

At every stage of the legal procedure, we can assist. In addition to discussing case, procedure, and process support, we also provide form assistance and statement writing assistance.

Our local constituency-County Courts from North

East Essex: **Email**

chelmsford@supportthroughcourt.org

Phone

0300 400 0141

Our phone line does not receive calls from withheld numbers. Please ensure that you are calling with your number available.

Office address

Support Through Court
Chelmsford County Court
Priory Place
New London Road
Chelmsford
Essex
CM2 0PP

Obviously your 'Support through Court' will have different contact details and addresses, and quite possibly different additional services that they each provide accordingly to their programme and staff that they attain equipped and trained for within office, having different variabilities in knowledge!

The Support through Court: Who we are

We empower people who face the courts alone

Every year, thousands of people in the UK face the courts alone. Often with no choice on their part, they must represent themselves at a moment that could determine the rest of their lives. They are at risk of divorce, being kicked out of the house or losing their children. In an unfamiliar courtroom, facing a party represented by an attorney, the process can be stressful and confusing.

We stand with those who have nowhere to turn.

We offer a free service across England and Wales, providing support and advice before, during and after court. We ensure that those facing court are not alone and help them navigate the complex legal system with dignity and confidence. Our nearly 500 volunteers help clients complete paperwork so they understand what they need to say in court and can best represent themselves. We ensure that people facing court alone feel prepared and supported to access justice.

Support through Court are a very dynamic organisation who support both mothers and fathers through parenting alienation, I must admit being the narrator here although I haven't included much about mothers facing parent alienation I am rather observant about how many mothers who become a parent alienated to their offspring also, which doesn't make it morally necessary or morally right, it's a trauma not only we face as parents but more importantly the child/children. Within their website they have a stories ribbon weblink, which provides many stories facing users from the Support Through Court, from the previous services users, which will give you a better insight, to who, why and where they support these people facing the injustice of things. Always remembering the Courts are there to try

and help you move forward, as they champion equalities, whilst trying to analyse maybe somewhat or not at all false allegations, or at least trying to understand the reason for separation, in many cases similar, alike may often become the stem from tradition narcissistic routes, but again that's not for us to judge that's for the judge and lawyers overseeing such a case.

The Support Through Court have services:

National helpline throughout the UK;

Birmingham-Cardiff-Chelmsford-Exeter-Leeds-

Liverpool-London-Manchester-NewcastleNewport-Nottingham-Sheffield-Southend

The services they can provide through the face for a family Court hearing: Remote hearing support during Coronavirus:

If you have an upcoming telephone or video hearing, one of our volunteers can help you.

Please contact our National Helpline on 03000

810 006

How we help with remote hearings:

We can support you with remote hearings in civil and family courts by discussing throughout the process, providing practical and procedural information as well as emotional support.

On the day of your remote hearing, we may attend the proceedings (by phone or video depending on which format the court has chosen). We may take brief, informal notes about what was said at the hearing and discuss it with you afterwards. Please note that we cannot provide you with legal advice or speak on your behalf at a hearing.

If you are concerned about your child/children's welfare, of where you believe parents are not fit for purpose, such as alcoholism, narcotics, domestic abuse or malnutrition, information providing you with here are NSPCC Services:

('NSPCC Every childhood is worth fight for!',

2023) Contact the NSPCC Helpline

You can contact the NSPCC Helpline by calling 0808 800 5000 or

emailing help@NSPCC.org.uk. Due to an increase in demand across our service, our voice Helpline is currently available 10am–8pm Monday to Friday. You can still email help@NSPCC.org.uk at any time for free, and you don't have to say who you are. If you think a child is in immediate danger, please call the police on 999 straight away.

If you are 18 or under?

Childline offers free, confidential advice and support whatever your worry, whenever you need help. 0800 1111

Within their website, at the top of their page has ribbon links that take you through the different services that they provide to guide you and your children.

(What is child abuse).

Types of abuse. Effects of child abuse. Reporting abuse.

Supporting signs of child abuse, Childrens stories. Our Services..

(Keeping children safe) Away from home supporting signs of child abuse. Sex and relationship. Children Mental health, Keeping children safe Online, Talking about drugs and alcohol, In the home, supporting for parents, reporting abuse, our services..

The NSPCC also hold charity events, where volunteers can participate to help raise awareness to their charitable Organisation: They withheld charity runs, cycling, charity treks, walks and challenge, dinners, balls and Galas.

As we are very near to the close of this journey, through the Court and other trials that you and your child/children would've been facing, I would like to wish you the best of luck, and just know that we have so much compassion for both mother and fathers who are separated from their offsprings, I hope the opposing parent starts to realise all the damage that it is also causing their child/children also. I started this journey to give you a guided support, and make you aware of the phycological trauma that you will be up against, this will help you prepare for what lie's before the courts and what lie ahead of the court hearings, your kid/kids it's a journey worth fighting for!

Through the Conclusion of Chapter 2

Throughout this chapter we have carefully narrated a discipline which will guide you through the Court scenario, We have entailed helpful guidance with the correspondence to the Judiciary reports/ such as section7/8/37/38 & PSO order, How to apply to the Court's, how to get legal advice, impartial advice, independent advice. What to expect from other Organisations such as CaffCass & Social Services, being prepared and able to answer every eventuality of your specific case. All the relevant links for your concerns have are there for your perusal and only you can deem what is relevant for you.

THE COME IN HANDY NOTABLE Dictionary Concepts & Meanings;

Tyranny-Dictatorship

Sovereignty- Supreme Power

Parliamentary—Governmental, congression, law making

Legislator- A person who makes laws, decisions- Politicians

Judicial- Involving a Law court

Actionable- Administrator- Court Material

Restraining order- Injunction-remand- Clarity

Purposive- Having done with a purpose

Teleological- Or finality is a reason or explanation for something in function of its end, purpose, or goal. It is derived from two

Greek words' Telos and Lagos

Proclamation- A public of official, a matter dealing with great importance.

Guillotine- Structure- blade to behead someone

Sporadic- Occurring at regular intervals or in a few places Prerogative- A right or privilege exclusive to a particular individual class.

Provocation- Action or speech that makes somebody angry Homicide- Killing of one person by another, i.e. murder executive or assassination

Lacuna- An unfilled space or gap

"Men's Rea"- An action or conduct which is a consent element of a crime as opposed to the mental state of the accused.

"Actus Reus" (in part) causing death

'Flux- The action or progress of flowing or flowing out. Necessity- The state of fact being required, the necessity of providing parental guidance! Bonafede- Genuine- Real

Flamboyant- Confidence- Stylish

Optimistic- Cheerful, cheery, positive, confident, hopeful

Philanthropist-Contributor, giver, sponsor, backer, healer

Prominent- Important-Famous

Reconciled- Restore friendly relations between

Forbearance- Patient self-control restraint and tolerance Perspective- Outlook, view, point of view, stance, attitude, approach

Atheist- Non believer- Un believer- sceptic-doubtful

Agnostic- Someone who does not know, or believes that it is impossible to know if god exists

Emasculate-Presence-Closeness

Postmodernism- Developed in mid to late 20th Century Compare- Estimate, measuring, or note the similarity or dissimilarity between

Contrast- The state of being strikingly different from something else in juxtaposition or close Association. "The day began cold and blustery, in contrast to almost two weeks of uninterrupted

sunshine's'.

Inequality- Difference in size, degree, Circumstances lack of equality

Equality- The state of being equal in rights or opportunities-

Male or female

Egalitarianism- The doctrine that people are equal and deserve equal rights and opportunities

Quantitative- Related to, measuring, or measured by the quantity of something rather than its quality

Qualitative- Relative to measuring, or measured by the quality of

something rather that it's quantity

Immigrant- A person who comes to live permanently in a foreign

Country

Migrant- A person who moves from one place to another, especially in order to find work or better living conditions asylum seeker a person who has left their Country as a Political refugee and is seeking asylum in another.

Cynicism- The belief that people are only interested in themselves and are not sincere

Apathetic- Showing or feeling no interest, enthusiasm, or concern Enfranchise- To endow with right, citizenship, especially the right to vote.

Disenfranchised- Depriving (Someone) of the rights to vote Scepticism- A sceptical attitude; doubt as to the truth of something!

An empirical study- is to make value

An normative study- is to make judgement about its importance Exemplified- To be or to give typical example of something Diversity- State of being diverse for different social background, ethnic, gender or sexual orientation

Inclusion- The aim of inclusion is to embrace all people irrespective or race, gender, disability, medical or other needs.

Reformism- is a political doctrine advocating the reform of an existing system or institution instead of it's abolition and replacement. The belief that gradual changes through and within existing institutions of a society can ultimately chance a society's fundamental economic relations.

Anarchism- belief, anarchism,[43]cluster[44]o[45]f doctrines and attitudes centred on the belief thatgovernment[46]i[47]s both harmful and unnecessary. Anarchist thought developed in the West and spread throughout the world, principally in the early 20th century. **Socialism- A Political and**

43. https://www.britannica.com/dictionary/cluster

44. https://www.britannica.com/dictionary/cluster

45. https://www.britannica.com/dictionary/cluster

46. https://www.britannica.com/topic/government

47. https://www.britannica.com/topic/government

economic theory of social organization which advocates that the means of production, distribution and exchange should be owned or regulated by the community as a whole.

Communism- A theory or system of social organisation in which all property is owned by the Community and each person contributes and receives according to their ability and needs. Liberalism- Is a Political and moral philosophy based on rights of the individual liberty, consent of the governed and equality before the law

Conservatism- is a cultural, social and Political philosophy that seeks to promote and preserve traditional social institutions and

practices. Socialism- The set of beliefs

that states that all people are equal and should share equally in a

Country's money, or Political systems based on these beliefs. Consensus- Is generally accepted opinion among a group of people.

Majoritarianism- Is a practise to which decisions of an organised group should be made by a numerical of its members. Globalisation- The increase of trade around the World especially by large companies producing and trading goods in many different countries.

Regionalism- A feeling of loyalty to a particular part of a country and wish for it to be more Political Independent!

Monsour- An Arabic name meaning 'he who is victorious. Emancipation. – Generally, means to free a person from a previous restraint or legal disability. More broadly it is also used for efforts to produce economic and Social Rights, Political Rights or equalities.

Hearth- As a brick stone, or concrete area infront of a fireplace or as the lowest section of the fireplace.

Heliocentrism- which means that the sun orbits at the centre of

the stars and earth! In acts 11:28 mentions Claudius Plutonomy and also fact. WWW.Space.Com/Heliocentrism[48] 1400 years ago. Nobility! The quality of being noble in character a man of nobility and learning! High class in the Country, the Aristocracy. Commoners, a commoner, also known as the

48. http://www.space.com/Heliocentrism

common man, commoners, the common people or the masses, an ordinary person in a community or nation who did not have any significant social status!

Grandiloquent- pompous or extravagant in language, style or manner, especially in a way that is intended to impress. Jolabokaflod- Iceland tradition in which books are given as a Christmas present and opened on December 24th, they spend the event reading books.

Obsolescence- The process of becoming obsolete or the condition of being nearly obsolete. Eudemonia- Happiness and well-being. Asunder- To break apart or to become parted, disunited or served!

(BIBLIOGRAPHY)

With climate change at thought and all the unique unnecessary with population growth national resource depletion, air pollution, national disasters such as war, the act of terrorism, global fires such as the latest in Australia, whirlwinds causing tornados, icebergs melting causing floods throughout towns and cities. Is this all a sign from God that humanity has become too hungry and insufficient? Through our National Politics, we support a wide range of institutions, including migrant and immigration control, land and sea management, air pollution, and the national environment. EU GDPR Regulations. Can someone genuinely take charge of what appears to be a massive Metropolitan lunatic institution in which we live amongst a greedy and demanding society, which can imply that few or many inside society become too mundane or too inebriated to realize how vital recycling is? How many babies have been obtained through intoxication? Let me start by saying that I am far from picture-perfect. I had numerous flaws from the age of 21 to 34 when I realized the value of adulthood and wanted to leave some kind of legacy. I also wrote Mind Matters I, Mind Matters II, and Criminal Minds Matter. I have a severe head injury that has caused me anxiety and sadness, as well as memory loss. I was violently beaten and assaulted by 15 men when I was only eighteen years old; I was left with a damaged eye socket and cheekbone, and my nose had been shoved into my brain, causing fluid to seep from my brain. Also, I have children whom I adore, and I have separated from my spouse, which has made seeing my children even more difficult. I am an estranged parent who suffers from secondary Reynaud's illness, which causes poor blood circulation in my hands and feet. like stone-dead cold. During the winter months, I can barely bear it feeling so isolated from a family orientated life.

https://www.amazon.co.uk/Mind.../dp/1471003[49]

752/ref=sr_1_4...[50]

https://www.amazon.co.uk/Mind.../dp/1471068[51]

528/ref=sr_1_3...[52]

https://www.amazon.co.uk/Crim.../dp/14710833[53]

---

49. https://www.amazon.co.uk/Mind%E2%80%A6/dp/1471003752/ref=sr_1_4%E2%80%A6
50. https://www.amazon.co.uk/Mind%E2%80%A6/dp/1471003752/ref=sr_1_4%E2%80%A6
51. https://www.amazon.co.uk/Mind%E2%80%A6/dp/1471068528/ref=sr_1_3%E2%80%A6
52. https://www.amazon.co.uk/Mind%E2%80%A6/dp/1471068528/ref=sr_1_3%E2%80%A6

65/ref=sr_1_2...[54]

https://www.barnesandnoble.com/.../the[5]
[5]mind.../1142610224...[5]
[7]https://www.barnesandnoble.com/.../mind.../11
[57]42254812...[58]The books can be found on both Amazon and Barnes & Noble.

Nursing Mental Health, acknowledge your wellbeing and the ones you care for. Tranquillity, peace, and rest. Sleep is very important in how we feel and act accordingly to our mood. If we are not sleeping, we become fatigued emotionless, and abrupt as our body tends to shut down.

Contributor Notes (464 / 2500)

Many people suffer from Mental Ill health, some have been suffering from birth with a diagnosis, and others formed from intoxication. Each and everyone deserves salivation & support

---

53. https://www.amazon.co.uk/Crim%E2%80%A6/dp/1471083365/ref=sr_1_2%E2%80%A6
54. https://www.amazon.co.uk/Crim%E2%80%A6/dp/1471083365/ref=sr_1_2%E2%80%A6
55. https://www.barnesandnoble.com/%E2%80%A6/the-mind%E2%80%A6/1142610224%E2%80%A6
56. https://www.barnesandnoble.com/%E2%80%A6/the-mind%E2%80%A6/1142610224%E2%80%A6
57. https://www.barnesandnoble.com/%E2%80%A6/mind%E2%80%A6/1142254812%E2%80%A6
58. https://www.barnesandnoble.com/%E2%80%A6/mind%E2%80%A6/1142254812%E2%80%A6

some of us need to make sacrifices of friends and social circles that don't bring to your table of salvation but rather than to have you suffer all the more. I really hope this book can give you a different outlook, mindset to life, as you deserve change, a second chance at life. Table of Contents (216 / 2500)

Impressionist Art Illustrations from ProcsArt

Published 08/2022 The Mind Matter by J.Johnson First Professional Revised Edition.

Health & Well-being Vitality Action-Plan

Categories and Keywords

Lulu Bookstore Category

Health & Fitness

BISAC Main Category

EDUCATION / Counselling / Academic

Development

BISAC Category 2

HEALTH & FITNESS / General

BISAC Category 3

HEALTH & FITNESS / Diet & Nutrition / General

Keywords

wellbeing, vitality, nutrition, mentality, plan, action, motivation, mind, matters. Audience

Professional and Scholarly – Adult audiences including professional development and academic research.

Our books are based on media studies, tabloids, broadsheet newspapers, human rights, and Law society, to guide you through courts. In court magistrates' hearings & sentencing. Crime bureau. How to stay on the right side of the Law.

Contributor Notes (170 / 2500)

This book is very fundamental, challenging different audiences such as college students, university students, and many adults who are thinking about joining the Law Society

Table of Contents (117 / 2500)

*Crimes & sentencing *Media studies *In court hearings and sentencing *family courts *help

through courts *Solicitors Categories and Keywords

Lulu Bookstore Category

Law

BISAC Main Category

LAW / Civil Rights

BISAC Category 2

BIOGRAPHY & AUTOBIOGRAPHY / Law

Enforcement

BISAC Category 3

LAW / Communications

Keywords

crime, law society, men's rea, actus reus, GBH,

ABH, narcotics, alcoholism, terrorism

Audience

Professional and Scholarly – Adult audiences including professional development and academic research.

The Truth of The Gospel [59]–[60]The Theophilus Of Christianity[61](wordpress.com)[62]

59. https://thetruthofthegospel4.wordpress.com/

60. https://thetruthofthegospel4.wordpress.com/

61. https://thetruthofthegospel4.wordpress.com/

62. https://thetruthofthegospel4.wordpress.com/

References

© 2023 FAMILY MEDIATION Council (2023) 'Families Mediation', *Family mediation council*, p.

1.

2023, L. (2023) 'Reports under section 37 of the Children Act 1989', *Reports under section 37 of the Children Act 1989*, p. 1.

'Alienated Mothers Retreat' (2023) *Family Seperation Clinic*, p. 1.

Astills, J. (2023) 'Section 7 Report', *Johnson Astills*, p. 1.

Clarke, D. (2023) *Single Parents familes in United Kingdom 1996/2022*. Available at: https://www.statista.com/statistics/281640/singl e-parent-families-uk/ (Accessed: 21 March 2023).

Court fees (2023) 'EX160 Help with court fees.', *Help with court fees*, p. 1.

Crown & database (2023) 'Section 38', *Family Law Act 1996*, p. 1.

Essex McKenzie Friend (2023) 'McKenzie Friend', *Mckenzie Friend Law Support*, p. 1.

Family Law, S. (2023) 'Family Mediators for Divorce', *Stow Family Law*, p. 1.

FNF.Org (2023) 'FNF.Org', *Families Nedd Fathers*, p. 1.

Gingerbread (2023) 'Single Parents day 2023', *Lewisham Children & Family Centres*, p. 1.

Jung, C. (2023) 'learning-mind.com/shadow-self', *Learning Mind*, p. 1.

'NSPCC Every childhood is worth fight for!' (2023) *NSPCC*, p. 1.

'Support through Family Court' (2023) *Support through Court*, p. 1.

Wolestonecraft, M. (1993) 'Reason & Sensibility/

The ideal for Womans Self Goverance/ In the

Writings of Mary Wolestonecraft', *Reason &*

Sensibility/ The ideal for Womans Self Goverance/ In the Writings of Mary Wolestonecraft, p. 1.

J.JOHNSONAUTHOR

About the Publisher

My academics is arts and humanities, (History & Politics), I've also studied also Mental Health and well-being in the work place and Mental Health wellbeing Advocacy. I am also Central Committee Representative for the Social Science and Arts Faculty. I have just recently I have expanded my writing, now with eleven published books. This is my latest Novel, such as a jurisconsult within the family Law disputes:

www.ingramcontent.com/pod-product-compliance
Lightning Source LLC
La Vergne TN
LVHW022117200926
848481LV00003B/1187
9798224883165